W9-DEL-308

SALT BEEF BUCKETS

BREAKWATER
P.O. Box 2188, St. John's, NL, Canada, A1C 6E6
WWW.BREAKWATERBOOKS.COM

A CIP catalogue record for this book is available
from Library and Archives Canada.

Copyright © 2021 Amanda Dorothy Jean Bulman

ISBN 978-1-55081-905-2

ALL RIGHTS RESERVED. No part of this publication
may be reproduced, stored in a retrieval system or
transmitted, in any form or by any means, without
the prior written consent of the publisher or a licence
from The Canadian Copyright Licensing Agency
(Access Copyright). For an Access Copyright licence,
visit www.accesscopyright.ca or call toll free
to 1-800-893-5777.

Canadä

Newfoundland
Labrador

We acknowledge the financial support of the Government
of Canada and the Government of Newfoundland and
Labrador through the Department of Tourism, Culture,
Industry and Innovation for our publishing activities.

PRINTED AND BOUND IN CANADA.

Breakwater Books is committed to choosing papers and materials for our
books that help to protect our environment. To this end, this book is printed
on a recycled paper that is certified by the Forest Stewardship Council®.

Amanda Dorothy Jean Bulman

SALT BEEF Buckets

A LOVE STORY

Recipes and Essays
Exploring the Stories
and Culinary Traditions
of Newfoundland

To my husband, who always believes in me; my family, especially my mom with her beautiful, warm heart; Nanny Bulman, whose pie crust and homemade bread are top shelf; and the good folks at CBC Newfoundland and Labrador who took a chance and published some of my work. Also, a big thank you to all the local fishers and farmers and gardeners and non-profit organizations for working towards food security solutions. A massive thank you to the Writers' Alliance of Newfoundland & Labrador (WANL) and Breakwater Books Ltd., without whom there would be no book. Finally, to my friend Veronica and her girlfriend Stacy, who sent me helpful and inspiring gifs throughout the process and tested a slew of the recipes.

I'd also like to acknowledge that, as a settler living on the ancestral lands of the Beothuk and Mi'kmaq, I am presenting the recipes and food traditions of the colonists who came to the island of Ktaqamkuk—what we call Newfoundland—and not the food traditions of the Indigenous peoples of the island.

INTRODUCTION

Hello! My name is Andie. I didn't always work in food; I went to school to be a librarian. I've always loved stories, so the library seemed like the perfect place for me. I quickly realized, however, that my energy level didn't match up with my chosen work. I'm hyperactive and social, and need something tactile, something that keeps me on my feet.

Instead of studying for my database management class, I spent my time making dips and homemade bread for my study group to eat. I catered events and parties at my school, and planned for weekend potlucks instead of studying. I did push through and finish my degree, but after graduation I took a job at a local bakery and learned how to make muffins, scones, homemade soups, biscuits, and big gooey brownies instead of seeking work in my field of study.

The bakery was where I started, but I have worked in different styles of food as well. I've done the fancy plated multi-course thing, and I've catered for oil companies that spared no expense. Even so, I knew that for me homemade stews, crusty bread, and chocolate chip cookies will always trump everything else. Making comfort food at a local bakery was work I could get behind. I made far less money, but each day was satisfying. While working in Halifax, I met my husband, a Newfoundlander; he wanted to be closer to friends and family, so after a brief deliberation period, we shoved all our worldly belongings into a U-Haul and drove onto the ferry.

When we left Halifax, the other cooks and bakers in my life sent me off with dire warnings. "Nothing grows there," "They boil everything to death," and "They only love white bread and seal flippers" were all ringing in my ears when we pulled up to our rental home in Pasadena, Newfoundland. I don't know if you've been to Pasadena, but it has to be the most fertile place on the island. I grew spinach, basil, beets, and more in my backyard flower beds. I could walk to two separate strawberry U-picks. My neighbours introduced themselves, and before I knew it they were dropping off fresh trout regularly. Other new friends gave us bottled moose to try. There was a fruit stand that sold juicy plums, just off the highway. Western Newfoundland is an oasis.

Our next move was to the Avalon Peninsula. The Avalon is an entirely different foodscape. I struggled to grow things in the heavy soil, and the winter seemed grey and endless, but the bogs and barrens have their own charms. I picked salt beef buckets full of blueberries; neighbours dropped off rabbits; Christmas dinner came with salt beef, boiled cabbage, and incredibly powerful slush. I took a job at the Reluctant Chef restaurant and learned how to use local ingredients in an entirely new way. I made friends with foragers and met some genuinely inspiring farmers—people who can take nothing and turn it into something.

Until the pandemic, I owned the Artist Café, a tiny space where I served seasonal comfort food to the staff and guests at the CBC, and catered events and art openings. The business did not survive COVID-19. It's hard to make money catering events when parties and plays aren't happening. Now, I have a day job, and I write articles about food, but when this is all over, I hope to return to making food and working with community groups like Agriculture in the Classroom NL and Little Green Thumbs.

SALT BEEF BUCKETS: A LOVE STORY is about my passion for the recipes of Newfoundland and Labrador. Initially, I wanted to write a book about the food history of this place. Can you imagine? That book would have weighed 800 pounds. The food history of Newfoundland and Labrador is one of the most complicated stories ever told. There would be villains, sea monsters, shipwrecks, rum-running, slave-trading, cod trawlers, fairies, ghosts, and recipes lost in time. I would need years to write that book, and even then, it would be incomplete.

I am thrilled that some good friends talked me out of that project. My next idea was to create a "cheffy" book that shows how traditional Newfoundland flavours can look in a contemporary restaurant setting; then Jeremy Charles released his giant, beautiful, and inspiring tome. So, back to the drawing board! What I finally decided on is a book that encompasses two things: traditional Newfoundland recipes (with a little history and folklore thrown in), and an updated, modern take on local food traditions that you can create in your own kitchen. There's nothing overly fancy about my interpretations on the standard fare; they're just a bit modernized, with some creative elements thrown in. I don't want you to be intimidated by the recipes, so I tried to keep things as simple as possible. I want this to be a book that gets pulled out frequently and is absolutely covered in stains. I want this book to be used!

SALT BEEF BUCKETS: A LOVE STORY celebrates local ingredients, researches archival recipes, and explores how the ways we use food are constantly changing and growing. It features recipes found in the archives—plucked out of old diaries, church fundraising books, and yellowed ancient letters—as well as my own updates to these recipes. I've organized it by season, reflecting the traditional patterns of food sourcing and usage—and I've included some side trips into other traditions as well, such as rug hooking, fairy lore, and how to build a fire! I've also invited some friends to contribute a recipe or two; I don't believe a book on the food of a place should come from just one person.

I don't think food recognizes borders, either, and I love that. It's something a chef told me early on in my career, and it's mostly true. I believe there is a tremendous amount of freedom in adapting recipes and making them your own. A dish might be born in one region, then move to another, with different people adding and subtracting from the recipe. The thing is, Newfoundland is almost an exception to this rule. Its physical isolation in the middle of the cold North Atlantic means that many of the recipes originating here have been left untouched by time. Oh, certain events did have an impact on local foodways: colonialism caused a tidal wave of change, as did entering into Confederation with Canada and the resettlement that followed. In more recent years, both the cod moratorium and the oil boom of the early twenty-first century have altered the culinary landscape as well. The history of food in Newfoundland is unique because it unfolded in isolation for so long, but rapid and exciting changes are now underway.

The border created by kilometres of cold ocean is less limiting now, so this book is a look backward and forward. I've dug up traditional recipes and stories, and I've updated them for a modern audience. I've added new ingredients and subtracted others. I've standardized recipes that gave measurements such as "a coffee cup of sugar." I interviewed hunters and anglers, chefs and home cooks. Still, there's much more I could and would have included; for example, I was unable to travel to Labrador because of the pandemic of 2020. There were negative effects on local food systems that I also didn't get to address because of the pandemic, such as invasive species in the bays and how chefs and fisher-folk will have to adapt, learning to eat and enjoy the bycatch, and finding ways to encourage Newfoundlanders to try new species.

On a more positive note, I was thrilled to write about how homesteading and small farms are becoming more and more prevalent here. There are also more gardens in elementary schools in Newfoundland than in any other province, and young children are learning about nutrition and gardening as part of their school curriculum through the program Little Green Thumbs. Foragers are getting creative and are picking and eating things that the first settlers left in the ground. Immigration is on the rise, too, which means we're gaining access to new culinary knowledge and tools. Many folks are bringing brilliant flavours into Newfoundland, and beautiful fusion cooking is happening all over!

As you read and use this book, I hope you'll enjoy the folklore and side trips, as well as some of the traditional recipes in their original wording (those aren't typos, they're old-timey style!). I've provided a reference list at the back for anyone interested in the people and publications that taught me some of these recipes, as well as some titles that I found informative or helpful. Occasionally, I've combined some of the traditional recipes to give you what I believe is the best version.

I hope you'll attempt to trek into the woods and have a boil-up. I hope you'll start seeds from scratch. Mostly, I want you to treat the recipes and ideas in the book like a road map. They are there to guide you, but recipes don't need to be rigid; wander off the path from time to time! You can add and change things where and when you want. Hopefully, the stories inspire you to make something warm and comforting, but more than that, I hope they inspire you to engage with the food scene all around you.

Andie

Late Winter
to Early Spring

In other parts of Canada, late winter and early spring are heralded by blossoming cherry trees, teenagers wearing shorts, and gardens being planted. Not here, though. Newfoundland and Labrador doesn't have many cherry trees, shorts stay packed away until July, and anything planted outside now would be dead by nightfall. This province does have one tradition that makes up for most of these seasonal shortcomings, though: spring in Newfoundland and Labrador is boil-up season.

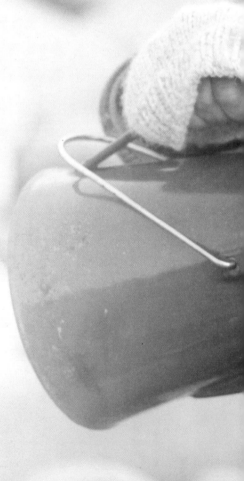

BOIL-UPS

From February to May, some of us trek into the woods, build fires, and sip tea mixed with tinned milk while huddling near a warming flame. I used to spend these months hiding in my house watching Netflix and working my way through a store aisle's worth of chip flavours. This is not the healthiest way to spend a season, so now every year I make a supreme effort to get out and make the most of the long season.

This tradition should be right up my alley—I'm a chef and I love smoky food. But the idea of lugging a bunch of cooking gear into the woods on my day off has prevented me from taking advantage of boil-up season in the past. I'm not from this province originally, so the term "boil-up" wasn't familiar to me. Neither was its cousin, the "mug up." I once accidentally confused the two at a party, only to be enthusiastically corrected by everyone there. Chastised, I reached out to Philip Hiscock, a retired folklore professor from Memorial University, to find out a bit more about the origins of these two expressions. I assumed mug ups had come from the British tradition of four o'clock tea time, but Hiscock set me straight, telling me that a century ago, fishing families would eat six or seven smaller meals over the course of a day at the height of the fishing season, fitting them in around the work from the early morning hours to the late evenings. "It is that sort of thing which is the grandparent of the modern mug up," Hiscock said. Interestingly, the boil-up seems to have an even longer history; he told me about a report from the 1600s of someone using "boil the kettle" as meaning "to have something to eat, including a cup of tea." This, of course, is still a widely used phrase in the province.

A boil-up is essentially a winter picnic in the woods or on a beach, and a mug up refers to taking a break to enjoy a cup of tea—kind of like the local version of the Swedish tradition of *fika*, which involves relaxing and enjoying a treat and warm beverage.

Armed with a little knowledge, I went into the woods with my friend Brendan Walsh. Brendan is a real expert, a keen fisherman, and an absolute genius at getting fires started. He has boil-ups several times a week throughout the winter and spring. He asked me to pick up matches, crusty bread, and water for the kettle, while he provided the mugs, plates, tea, cans of beans, hotdogs, tinned milk, and a beautiful cast-iron kettle. That sounds like a lot of gear, but it all fit into one bag. As we hiked, we chatted and gathered dry scraps of wood. Once we found the spot, I sat and tried to calm my dog—keen on the scent of rabbits—while Brendan built the fire.

Everything was vaguely smoky, the bread was lightly toasted, and I've never had a better cup of tea. Boil-ups are a proud Newfoundland and Labrador tradition. They are infinitely better than most everything on Netflix and are only a little harder to execute than firing up a binge-watch. Since this trip, I've tried to get into the woods and have a boil-up as often as possible. Spending time in the woods just feels good. On that note, before I get into the late winter and early spring recipes, I want to quickly describe the best way to start a fire. Over the past few years, my fire-starting skills have greatly improved! For lots of folks, the idea of starting a nice fire for a cook-up is intimidating. Here's how to make it simple.

FIRE-STARTING 101

Starting a fire is easy, but like most new things it can seem daunting! You'll need the following supplies:

> A pile of **rocks**.

> **Matches** or some other kind of fire starter. No lighter fluid please—you'll burn someone's house down and your marshmallows will taste weird.

> **Tinder**. You can't swipe right on this. It's essential! Tinder means tiny branches, dried leaves, old newspaper. Tinder gets the fire going!

> **Kindling**. Make sure your kindling is dry! Kindling is generally wood that's a little thicker than tinder, but not as thick as logs—maybe two-fingers-width thick.

> **Logs**. I mean, I don't need to explain this, do I? You can bring your own, but hunting for old wood in the wilderness is part of the fun.

> **Water**, for dousing your fire!

First, check to make sure conditions are right for a fire. I usually have boil-ups on a rocky beach, but there's nothing wrong with tea in the woods. In late March to early May, you'll probably be okay in the woods, but in August you're going to want to avoid everything but a good beach fire. Forest fires are no joke, so take no chances. Next, you need to pick your spot and begin building a small firepit. Just pick an area of flat ground away from trees. To stop the wood from falling apart into the area where you're sitting, dig a small hole and surround it with rocks.

Start with tinder; put some in the centre of your firepit. Remember, tinder is the small sticks, twigs, and leaves you're

going to use to get your fire burning, so dryness is key! One friend always brings dryer lint, which can be useful as a fire starter. Next, stack the kindling on top of the tinder; I usually make a cone-shaped structure. Finally, grab your matches and light the tinder. It helps to light it in a few different places to get it burning faster. Note that you may need to add more tinder if the kindling takes a while to catch fire. As the fire burns, you can gradually build it up by adding larger and larger logs. When you're ready to move on, douse that flame entirely with water, and smother it with earth. Don't you dare leave even a single glowing ember!

BREADS AND BAKED GOODS

On to the cooking! I try my best to cook seasonally, so recipes for berries and mushrooms reside in the Fall section, and nettles and the like are found in Mid-Spring to Summer. Late Winter to Early Spring is bread season. At this time of year, I'm yearning for kinder, more manageable weather, and I take my anxiety out on various bread doughs, pounding and kneading as I wait for the temperature to climb. In my archival adventures, I found reference to a "Big Bread Baking Competition" in Carbonear on April 17, 1937; I'm going to take this as evidence that Newfoundlanders in previous decades also saw this time of year as bread season. I tried to track down the winning recipe but only reached dead ends, so I turned to tomes and articles for bread inspiration.

Fatback and molasses are words that loom large in Newfoundlanders' collective imagination, so I started with a recipe that combines these flavours. The cookbook by the same name continues to fly off the shelves, and it stands as a perfect snapshot of time and life in Newfoundland during the late 1960s. I didn't find this recipe in that trusted volume, however. I found it tucked into an old fire department fundraising cookbook, but then I discovered that it's also in *Fat-Back and Molasses* under the name "pork toutens." Some of these old recipes show up in dozens of cookbooks under a plethora of names.

Molasses Pork Loaf 2.0 | page 25

Molasses bread is a long-time favourite for fishers, sealers, and other maritime folks. They used to take lassy bread with them on long journeys and eat it with crispy fatback tucked into the middle of the bread. This treat was often served with milky tea or a shot of whisky—giving them strength and warmth and something to look forward to on their long days. The original lassy and pork bun recipe I found is just below. It has unclear instructions and a disturbing amount of salt pork, and you have to eyeball the amount of water! Don't get me wrong—this recipe works; it just needed some love.

Old-School Lassy Buns and Salt Pork
(Makes 12 to 14 buns)

4 cups flour
1/2 tsp baking soda
1/2 tsp baking powder
1 cup molasses
1 lb salt pork, chopped and minced
water

Mince or chop pork and place in hot water to remove some of the salt. Let stand for five minutes. Sift dry ingredients. Remove pork from water and add to molasses. Add flour mixture to molasses mixture, alternatively with water to make a soft dough. Pat out on floured board and cut into pieces. Bake at 400F for 20 to 25 minutes.

My updated version uses far less fatback. I've also added toasted oats for fibre and flavour. There is something incredibly tempting about the smell of toasted oats on a cast-iron pan. I also cut back on the amount of salt pork, for heart health, and I went for a loaf instead of buns. I used Crosby's Fancy Molasses, a local favourite. Both recipes are excellent boil-up fare. I also like to serve it alongside moose sausages, to soak up all the syrupy goodness that leaks out of the meat.

Molasses Pork Loaf 2.0

MAKES 1 LOAF

2 ½ cups flour

2 tsp baking powder

2 tsp baking soda

1 cup large flake oats, toasted

½ cup brown sugar

2 tbsp finely diced salt pork

¼ cup canola oil

1 large egg

½ cup fancy molasses

1 ¼ cups water

Preheat oven to 350°F and grease a loaf pan. Combine flour, baking powder, and baking soda, and whisk well. Toast the oats on medium heat in a frying pan. Once they are a nice golden brown, add the toasted oats and brown sugar to the flour mixture and stir. Sauté the salt pork in the same pan used for the oats, until it's gorgeously caramelized.

Add the cooked salt pork, oil, egg, molasses, and water into the dry ingredients, and stir until everything is wet and evenly incorporated. Pour into greased bread pan and bake 50 minutes or until an inserted toothpick comes out clean. Let cool for 5 minutes, then remove from pan.

TEA BUNS AND TEA BISCUITS

Newfoundland is the tea biscuit province. Raisin tea biscuits, blueberry biscuits, cheddar biscuits, and plain can be found at almost every tiny corner store. I like my tea biscuits to be tall, layered, and flaky, and I want a touch of honey in them!

As part of my job with CBC's *Food and Fun* I get to interview bakers, foragers, and chefs. As a result, I can declare that the best bakery tea biscuits in the province belong to Wanda in Small Point, Newfoundland. It's worth the drive just to taste them; her recipe is tea bun perfection. She wouldn't share the secret with me (I don't blame her), but the second recipe below is my best attempt at replicating it. The other recipe is an amalgamation of tea bun recipes that I found in old spiral-bound church cookbooks. Both recipes are beautiful in their own way, and I think they both reflect their eras.

Andie's Version of Old-School Newfoundland Tea Biscuits

MAKES 10 BISCUITS

3 cups flour

1 tsp salt

5 tsp baking powder

½ cup butter

¼ cup sugar

1 cup milk

1 egg, beaten

Preheat oven to 425°F. Combine flour, salt, and baking powder in a bowl. Rub in butter until the mix looks like fine breadcrumbs. Stir in sugar, blending well. Combine milk and egg in a separate bowl. Stir well and fold into the dry ingredients. Combine the whole thing into a ball. Knead, but don't overmix. Roll out dough with a pin until about half an inch thick. Cut out with a glass. Bake for 20 minutes.

Modernized Honey Buttermilk Biscuits

MAKES 8 BISCUITS

Lots of coffee shops and small bakeries use whipping cream or coffee cream in their biscuits. I'm not a fan. It might sound a tad snobby, but I think that buttermilk is the only real option here; buttermilk adds a tart sourness that biscuits need. Another tip? I want that butter cold! Stick it in the freezer for an hour before using—preferably even longer. Grate it with the cheese grater! Don't overmix the dough—your biscuits will be hard and disappointing. Don't twist the biscuit cutter either; this deflates the whole thing. Bake your biscuits so that the sides are touching; this will force them to grow tall and beautiful.

2 ⅓ cups flour

2 tbsp baking powder

2 tsp salt

½ cup unsalted butter, very cold and grated

1 cup + 2 tbsp cold buttermilk

2 tsp honey

Honey Butter Glaze (optional, see recipe below)

Preheat oven to 425°F and line a baking sheet with parchment paper. **NOTE:** *You can use a well-oiled cast-iron pan instead.* Place the flour, baking powder, and salt together in a large bowl and whisk well. Grate the frozen butter into the mixture using a box grater. Make a well in the centre of the mixture. Pour all the buttermilk into the well, then add the honey. Stir everything together until just about combined; do not overwork the dough. The dough will be very crumbly.

Turn the dough out onto a lightly floured work surface and gently mould it into a rectangle using your hands. Don't over-mix, but combine. Gently roll the dough out with a rolling pin until it is about an inch thick. Cut into 3-inch circles. Don't twist your cutter! Arrange in a 10-inch cast-iron pan or close together on the lined baking sheet. Brush the tops with honey butter glaze, if using. Bake for 15 minutes or until biscuits are golden brown on top. Remove from the oven and, if desired, brush with more honey butter glaze. Let cool and eat.

Honey Butter Glaze

MAKES ENOUGH TO GLAZE 8 BISCUITS

2 tbsp melted butter

1 tbsp honey

Mix together for gorgeous honey butter.

POTATO BISCUITS, POTATO ROLLS, AND BOXTY

Various takes on potato-infused bread, pancakes, and biscuits can be found in a slew of Newfoundland cookbooks and newspapers. It's difficult to trace these recipes, but we can probably assume that the idea of mashing or grating potato into bread comes from Northern Ireland, where farls (almost like an English muffin) and boxty (potato pancakes) abound. Both dishes are thought to originate from the days of the Irish famine and were presumably created to make the potatoes and flour stretch as far as possible in that time of great need. Like any of the bread recipes in this chapter, these are more than suitable for year-round consumption. I just felt like root vegetables and St. Patrick's Day made them ideal for this chapter.

Andie's Version of Traditional Potato Biscuits MAKES 12 BISCUITS

6 to 8 medium potatoes

1 cup milk or cream

1 tbsp melted butter

Salt, to taste

½ cup flour

1 tbsp baking powder

Preheat oven to 400°F and line a baking sheet with parchment paper. Boil and mash the potatoes, making sure they are free of lumps.

Add the milk, butter, and salt. Add the baking powder and just enough flour—approximately ½ cup—to make a soft dough, then lay it on a floured board and roll it out quickly and lightly into a half-inch-thick sheet. Cut into rounds; arrange on baking sheet and bake about 10 minutes, or until just crisp on the outside. Butter and eat before they fall.

TIP > I don't peel the potatoes. The skin gives the biscuits added fibre and flavour, and you hide all manner of sin if you call something "rustic."

Potato Biscuits 2.0

MAKES 8 ROLLS

Commercial yeast was not widely available to rural folks in Newfoundland for many decades. Hence, the majority of older potato-bread recipes don't call for yeast. I added some here, along with rosemary and caraway seeds. This is a pretty great winter treat. I like serving this alongside a beet soup.

¼ cup water, slightly warmed

1 ½ tsp instant dry yeast

¼ cup sugar, divided

½ cup mashed potatoes

¼ cup milk

3 tbsp salted butter, melted and cooled

1 large egg

1 tbsp garlic powder

¾ tsp salt

2 ½ to 3 cups flour

Sea salt, to taste

1 tsp caraway seeds

1 ½ tbsp fresh rosemary leaves, chopped

In the bowl of a stand mixer, combine the slightly warmed water, the yeast, and half a teaspoon of the sugar. Set aside for about 5 minutes, until it looks good and bubbly. Add the remaining sugar, mashed potatoes, milk, butter, egg, garlic powder and salt to the bowl with the yeast mixture and stir with a spatula until smooth. Add the flour and mix until you form a shaggy dough—loose, with threads of flour, and lumpy but well mixed.

With a dough hook attachment on the stand mixer set to low, or on the counter if kneading by hand, knead for 7 minutes until the dough is smooth, forms a ball around the dough hook, and pulls away from the sides of the bowl.

TIP > If the whole thing is too sticky, add a bit more flour—not too much, though!

Place the dough in a lightly greased bowl, cover with plastic wrap, and allow to rise somewhere warm for about 2 hours.

Lightly grease a 13×9-inch baking dish and line it with parchment paper. When the dough has risen, turn it out onto a lightly floured surface and cut into 8 pieces. Roll each piece into a small ball and place seam-side down in the baking dish. Cover with a tea towel and let the rolls rise until puffed and nearly doubled in size, about an hour and a half.

Preheat oven to 375°F. Brush the tops of your rolls with about a tablespoon of melted butter, and then sprinkle with sea salt, caraway seeds, and rosemary. Place in oven and bake for about 15 to 20 minutes.

I like to serve these with a beet soup or lobscouse.

1939 Potato Pancakes or Boxtys

MAKES ABOUT 8 PANCAKES OR BOXTYS

Boxty on the griddle,
Boxty in the pan,
if you can't make Boxty,
you'll never get a man.

TRADITIONAL IRISH RHYME

4 large potatoes

2 tbsp flour

2 eggs

½ tsp salt

8 strips of cooked bacon

Butter to grease pan

The Presbyterian Ladies Aid (P.L.A.) published several cookbooks, and they have been an incredible aid to me. Like *Fat-Back and Molasses*, they serve as a perfect window into the past. Most editions of their cookbooks have some version of a potato pancake nestled into the bread section. Potato pancakes are pretty much just a recipe for boxty—a quintessential Irish dish. A boxty is a sort of combination hash brown and potato scone. It is a great way to use potatoes, makes for excellent St. Paddy's Day morning fare, and pairs well with just about anything. I like it with smoked trout and a little green salad. The little poem above is kind of a bummer, but it highlights just how vital the dish was to the Irish. This boxty recipe didn't come from any one source, but was inspired by all the potato pancake recipes in the P.L.A. cookbooks.

Peel potatoes and grate. Add flour, eggs, and salt. Mix well. Drop on hot buttered pan and fry until a crisp golden brown.

Serve small pieces of bacon between two potato pancakes.

Modern Twist: Sweet Potato Boxty

MAKES ENOUGH FOR 12 PANCAKES

I love sweet potatoes. I know they aren't traditional Newfoundland fare, but sweet potato boxty served alongside pickled blueberries, bottled moose, and maybe a fried egg would be a real breakfast of champions!

2 cups flour

1 tsp baking powder

1 tsp salt

1 cup boiled and mashed sweet potato

1 ½ cups grated raw sweet potato

1 cup buttermilk

Butter for the pan

In a small bowl, combine flour, baking powder, and salt, mix well, and set aside. Using a large mixing bowl, combine the mashed sweet potatoes with the raw, grated sweet potato, then add the flour mixture and mix together. Make a little well and slowly pour in your buttermilk. Now, get your best cast-iron pan nice and hot. Add a pat of butter to the pan. Scoop out some batter, shape it into a nice patty, and put it in the pan. Cook for 4 minutes, then flip and cook the other side for 4 minutes, then serve. Voilà!

HARD-TACK: A HISTORY

It's tricky to know where to discuss hard-tack because it seems like it's more of a ration or ingredient than an actual dish. Hard-tack is still standard fare for fishers and sealers, and their season starts in early spring. It goes by many names: ship's biscuit, pilot bread, and sea bread were some polite ones. Molar breakers, dog's biscuits, worm castles (as it frequently contained weevils), and sheet iron were a few others.

Hard-tack usually has only three ingredients—flour, water, salt—it's a hard, dry cracker. It came to Newfoundland via European fishers and traders. Hard-tack was vital on long sea voyages; since refrigeration was non-existent and sea travel often took months, hard-tack was often the mainstay of sailors' diets. Little wonder that scurvy was so prevalent; hard-tack is pretty devoid of nutrition; its value is as a filler of stomachs and little else.

Hard-tack wasn't unique to the British navy. The history of this so-called food stretches back as far as ancient Egypt. Different cultures have put their own spin on the dish; Roman sailors had an exciting version called *bucellatum*, which was made by mushing together a paste of wheat flour and water that was then dried, hardened, sliced, and fried. It was served with honey and pepper.

Andie's Version of Traditional Hard-Tack

MAKES ABOUT 1 SHEET PAN OF HARD-TACK

Out on the water, hard-tack is usually enjoyed with a cup of hot tea. On land, Newfound-landers use hard-tack in classic meals such as fish and brewis. Purity Factories, a New-foundland company, started mass-producing it in the 1950s, but as with most things, hard-tack is better when it is homemade, so here's my old-school recipe. Making it from scratch might seem a bit extra, but it will improve your fish and brewis tenfold, and it does have a certain charm when dipped in soup, tea, or beer.

4 ½ cups flour

3 tbsp salt

1 ½ cups water

Preheat the oven to 375°F. Add flour and salt to a mixing bowl.

TIP > The amount of water you need can vary a bit, so I add half a cup at a time and work it in.

Knead the dough; the final consistency you are going for is just pliable enough to be smooth and worked with a rolling pin. Roll out till approximately 1 inch thick. Cut into square biscuit shapes. Poke holes in the dough. Bake in the oven for 30 to 40 minutes. Allow to cool completely before eating.

Top-Notch Cracker or "Hard-Tack" with Summer Savoury

MAKES 1 SMALL BATCH OF CRACKERS

Hard-tack is a bit like a cracker, so here's an even better recipe that reads more like something to put on a late winter/early spring cheeseboard.

1 ½ cup flour

2 tsp dried summer savoury

1 tsp black pepper

1 ½ tsp salt

1 tsp sugar

2 tbsp olive oil

½ cup cold water

1 tbsp sea salt

Preheat oven to 450°F. Line a baking sheet with parchment paper. Pulse the flour, savoury, black pepper, salt, sugar, and the olive oil in the food processor until evenly distributed.

Add the water and pulse just until the dough starts to stick together, about 10 seconds. Remove the dough, press together gently with your hands to form a single ball, and cut into four pieces. Let the dough rest for about 10 minutes.

Sprinkle a little bit of flour onto your counter and roll out each ball of dough as thin as you possibly can. Once they are flat, place each piece of dough on the baking sheet. Brush them with about a tablespoon of olive oil and top with some good quality flaky sea salt.

Bake for 4 to 5 minutes but check periodically to make sure they're not getting too brown. Flip each cracker piece and bake for another 4 to 5 minutes.

Turn the oven off and let the crackers sit in the oven for 1 to 2 hours so that they really dry out and get crispy.

GINGER CAKE

Gingerbreads and cakes pop up in most older Newfoundland cookbooks, which I adore, since a big slice of ginger cake is just the thing for the last of those winter storms. I found these first two recipes in the *Ladies College Aid Society Cookbook*. This is a rare collection of recipes from 1905 that lives in the Newfoundland and Labrador Provincial Archives. The first recipe is a pretty standard ginger cake, but with some hilarious measurements. The second recipe is an add-on!

Old-School Ginger Cake

Four cups flour, one pint molasses, one pound butter warmed with the molasses, five eggs, one cup of boiled apple, ginger and mixed spices to taste, one cup brown sugar, one cup raisins. The above recipe will make a large ginger cake.

A TRAMP WITH A SILK HAT ON

Instead of baking your gingerbread in the ordinary square pans, pour the batter into two layer-cake pans, then as soon as it cools dress it with a coconut frosting. The sweetness of the icing seems to dispel a certain bitter flavor given to the gingerbread by the molasses.

New-School Ginger Cake

MAKES ONE 10-INCH CAKE

In this recipe, I've added fresh grated ginger, a lime syrup, and some apples to add moisture.

1 cup grated fresh ginger

1 apple, grated (I like to use Gala or Honeycrisp)

1 cup sugar

1 cup canola oil

1 cup molasses

1 tsp cinnamon

1 tsp cardamom

1 tsp ginger

½ tsp cloves

2 tsp baking soda

2 tsp salt

¼ tsp black pepper

2 ⅓ cups all-purpose flour

1 cup boiling water

3 eggs

Preheat oven to 350°F. Grease a 10-inch round cake pan and line with parchment paper. Grind the ginger, apple, and sugar together in a food processor. Pour this mixture into the bowl of a stand mixer. Add canola oil and molasses. Mix at medium speed for 3 minutes. In a separate bowl, mix all the spices, baking soda, salt, pepper, and flour together. Take a moment to really sift this well, then set aside.

Next, turn the mixer back on at a very, very low speed. Add the cup of boiling water, being careful not to burn yourself. Once the water has been incorporated into the sugar/apple/ginger/oil/molasses mixture, make a well in the bowl of dry ingredients and pour in the mixture. Add the eggs one at a time, mixing between each egg. **NOTE:** *The batter is going to seem absurdly thin, but don't worry.*

Pour into the cake pan and bake for 40 minutes. Test your cake using a toothpick, and leave in for 5 more minutes if needed.

Once cool, dress with a lime glaze (see recipe below).

Lime Glaze

MAKES ENOUGH GLAZE FOR ONE 10-INCH CAKE

1 cup powdered sugar

2 ½ tbsp fresh lime juice

1 tsp lime zest

Just mix it all together and make those clumps disappear.

Enjoy a big slice of ginger cake with a big cup of dark coffee, a mystery novel, and a late-in-the-season snowstorm.

SOUPS

LOBSCOUSE

Lobscouse is a dish that pops up all over Newfoundland, but it's also found around the world. There's an English version that was and continues to be immensely popular with Liverpool dockworkers and sailors. Norway has a stew called *lapskaus*, which is like our version but sometimes contains fermented cabbage (which I was VERY inspired by). The Germans also have *lapskaus*, but theirs is more like a hash than a stew. Fishers and sailors who eventually settled in camps along Newfoundland's coast probably brought the recipes with them from their native countries.

It gained popularity because it was a cheap meal that could stretch to feed a big family. There's even a tiny inlet named "Lobscouse Cove" here in Newfoundland. Some folks hate lobscouse, and I get it. I've had bland versions. In 1707 satirist Edward Ward mentioned lobscouse in a letter and wrote that "He has sent the fellow to the devil, that first invented lobscouse."

Personally, I see it as something of a blank canvas. I've listed a plain version below, but I have also included a recipe for a funkier modern version, using toasted fennel seeds and caraway. Furthermore, I took a note from the Scandinavians and used sauerkraut instead of cabbage. I wanted something fresh, so I topped it with microgreens. Also, I didn't use salt beef. While I am a fan, stewing beef just tasted better to me. Try both recipes and let me know which you like!

The first recipe comes from my mother-in-law. You'll notice there's not much in the way of instructions; that's because she learned from her mother-in-law, who was an excellent cook, but not necessarily one for writing things down. This recipe didn't come with any instructions, so I boiled everything together and it worked out great.

Old-School Lobscouse (Makes enough for 4 to 6 people)

6 cups water	1 cup turnip, chopped	1 medium carrot, chopped
1 1/2 cup broth	1/2 cup cabbage, chopped	1 celery stalk
1 cup salt beef	1 medium potato, chopped	1 tsp black pepper
2 onions, chopped		sea salt

Lobscouse 2.0

MAKES ENOUGH FOR 4 TO 6 PEOPLE

2 tbsp cornstarch

1 tbsp salt

2 ½ cups beef, cubed

1 tbsp canola oil

2 medium carrots, peeled and chopped

1 onion, diced

2 small leeks, trimmed and sliced

3 sprigs fresh thyme

2 ½ cups potatoes, peeled

4 cups beef stock

dash Worcestershire sauce

1 tbsp (or to taste) sauerkraut, to garnish (optional)

1 tbsp toasted caraway, to garnish (optional)

2 tsp toasted fennel seeds, to garnish (optional)

Fresh dill or microgreens, to garnish (optional)

Preheat oven to 325°F. Take the cornstarch and salt and mix them in a bowl. Toss your beef in this cornstarch mixture. It might seem unorthodox, but it is going to give your beef a nice appealing crust and texture. Grab a frying pan or sturdy stewpot, heat over medium, and add the canola oil. Once the oil is heated, throw that beef on the heat for about 4 or 5 minutes until it's nice and brown. Add the carrots, onion, leeks, and thyme to the pan.

GET AHEAD! While the carrots and other vegetables are cooking, take the time to roast your potatoes!

Cube the potatoes into ½-inch pieces, toss and coat with olive oil, season with salt and pepper, and stick them on a baking sheet. They should roast in the oven for about 30 minutes, or until they get a beautiful colour. Get those roasted potatoes into the stewpot with everything else, then pour the stock into the pot along with the Worcestershire.

I would cook the stew for about an hour. Grab a book and a glass of wine and make sure you get up now and then to give the whole thing a stir. You can play around here, adding more broth or less, depending on how thin or thick you want your lobscouse. Garnish with sauerkraut, toasted caraway and fennel seeds, dill, and/or microgreens.

NEWFOUNDLAND PEA SOUP

It took me a while to come around to pea soup, but now it is a favourite. I found this particular pea soup recipe in an older, out-of-print Presbyterian Ladies Aid cookbook from 1924. I love the instructions; they aren't rigid, just chop it up and throw it in. There's no ingredient list, just what's in the directions.

Old-School Newfoundland Pea Soup
(Makes enough for 4 to 6 people)

Liquor from one ham bone (1 qt.), 1 cup milk, 2 cups peas boiled until soft, and mashed through a strainer. One tablesp butter, pepper to taste and salt if necessary. Thicken with a little flour wet with water. Cook till thick.

Andie's Version of Newfoundland Pea Soup Dumplings

MAKES ENOUGH DUMPLINGS FOR 6 SERVINGS OF SOUP

While the recipe above is from an older cookbook, the dumplings are standard fare, a combination of dumpling recipes that I came across.

2 cups flour

4 tsp baking powder

½ tsp salt

1 tbsp butter

1 cup water

Mix all of the dry ingredients together. Rub cold butter into the dry ingredients. Gradually add water. Shape the dough with your hands.

TIP > You can use a biscuit cutter to make small dumplings, but I tend to just plop the whole thing on top of the soup for about 15 minutes.

Moose Stew MAKES ENOUGH FOR 4 TO 6 PEOPLE

There are dozens of moose stew recipes in old Newfoundland cookbooks, and almost all of them are gems. I didn't include an archived recipe here, because my modernized version is already so similar to what you might find. Old recipes for moose stew are for large families, so I downsized this one, added sautéed kale as a garnish, tossed in some delicious garlic, and deglazed the pan with red wine. I haven't reinvented the wheel here, because some recipes are already perfect.

1 ½ lbs moose roast

2 tbsp cornstarch

Salt and pepper, to taste

3 tbsp butter

2 onions, diced

3 carrots, peeled and chopped

2 celery stalks, chopped

2 tsp chopped fresh parsley

6 cloves garlic, minced

4 tbsp tomato paste

½ cup red wine

4 cups beef stock/broth

2 bay leaves

1 cup red-skinned baby potatoes, quartered or halved

2 tsp salt

1 ¼ tbsp apple cider vinegar

½ cup sautéed kale (optional)

Using a very sharp knife, cut your moose into nice even pieces, about 1 ½-inch chunks. Pat them dry. Don't fool around and skip this step; dryer meat means you'll get a better sear! Toss your moose chunks into the cornstarch and season with salt and pepper. Heat some butter in a pan. **NOTE:** *Lots of recipes will claim that this step should be done with oil because butter burns. There's something to that, but I find that if you work quickly and efficiently, the butter just kind of browns nicely and gives a little sweetness to the moose.*

Sauté over medium-high heat until you see a nice sear. **NOTE:** *Don't overcrowd the pan; fry the moose pieces in batches.* Wipe the pan with paper towel in between each batch. Add more butter as needed.

In a separate large soup pot, sauté onion, carrots, and celery over medium heat for about 5 minutes and let them cook. You want your onions to be translucent, or even a little caramelized. Add fresh parsley and garlic in the last minute of sautéing. Now add your moose pieces to the pot. Stir in tomato paste and cook for 1 minute. Deglaze the pan with the wine. Let this all cook together for a few minutes. Now, add beef stock, bay leaves, potatoes, and about 2 teaspoons of salt. Cook for 1 hour at medium heat with lid on. Stir occasionally! In the last 10 minutes, add apple cider vinegar. In the last 5 minutes, sauté your chopped kale in a pan with some butter and salt, if you're using it as a garnish.

I like to serve this with dark rye bread, a green salad, and a good glass of red wine.

Kik Alicha

MAKES ENOUGH FOR 4 TO 6 PEOPLE

After interviewing Mimi Sheriff for CBC's *Food and Fun*, I knew I had to ask her to contribute a recipe for this book. Mimi owns Gursha, Newfoundland's first Ethiopian catering company, and she makes some of my favourite food in the province. Mimi excels at slow-cooked stews and meaty *tibs* (slow-roasted or braised meat stew) that she serves atop spongy sour *injera*, a traditional sourdough-type pancake, but it's her vegan recipes that I covet most! Kik Alicha is a comforting and flavourful split-pea stew, and I think it'll ring familiar to many Newfoundlanders. Typically eaten with *injera*, it can also be enjoyed with rice and a side of your favourite greens.

1 ½ cups split yellow peas, washed thoroughly

¼ cup canola oil

2 large red or yellow onions, finely chopped

1 tbsp grated garlic

1 tbsp grated ginger

2 tsp turmeric

3 or 4 cups warm water

1 ½ tsp salt

Chopped jalapeño (optional)

Rinse and drain the split yellow peas. Bring a medium pot of water to a boil and add the split yellow peas. Parboil the peas for about 30 minutes; you want the consistency to be lightly mashed. In a separate pot, heat the oil and add the onion. Cook for 15 minutes until light brown and translucent. Add the garlic and ginger to the onion, lower the temperature, and cook for a further 10 minutes, stirring frequently to ensure that the onion does not burn. Add the turmeric and stir for a minute or so, adding a tablespoon of water.

Strain the peas and keep about 1 cup of the remaining water. Add the peas to the onions and stir in the remaining water, bringing the mixture to a simmer for 5 minutes. If you don't have any remaining water from the boiled peas, add an additional 1 cup of warm water. Add the salt and stir in an additional 2 cups of warm water, then put on the lid and let the sauce simmer for 10 to 15 minutes. **NOTE:** *You want the final consistency to have a bit of texture from the peas and be easily pourable but not runny.*

Remove from heat to serve and add freshly chopped jalapeño on top for a bit of spice.

Juniper Apple Soup

MAKES ENOUGH FOR 6 TO 8 PEOPLE

This recipe comes from Malin Enström. I want to be her when I grow up. I've had the privilege of living next to Malin and her family for the last four years, and I've loved every second. First, this is a whole family of lifelong learners. Everyone is constantly trying something new: biking, growing tea gardens, foraging. I am so inspired by the way they live. Also, Malin is an incredible visual artist. I remember walking around The Rooms and staring at this substantial matted rug and wondering who had created such an exciting beauty, only to read the little tag and realize it was Malin. During Snowmaggedon, she dropped off a bottle of wine for me, which after a week of shovelling felt like the work of an angel. Malin's from Sweden, and because of the way she talks about that magnificent country, I'm saving for a trip. I was so excited to ask her for this recipe. Here are her words:

> My favourite Swedish chef, Marcus Samuelsson, inspired me with one of his recipes from the book Aquavit, and this soup comes from that idea. Juniper has always been a big part of my life, as it is a common evergreen in the archipelago where I grew up. It is also a part of my name: En-ström means "juniper stream" in Swedish. I adore its long, trailing branches, its scale-like needles, its pretty and flavourful berries, and, of course, its aromatic wood, regardless of the season. This is a soup that speaks to my heart when I miss home, through scent and taste both. The juniper berries have a wild, piney, resinous flavour that is perfectly paired with the apple. It stands alone as a lovely soup but can also be paired with wild game dishes, such as moose, to become an unexpected fusion between Newfoundland and Sweden cuisine—the best of (my) two worlds.

1 tbsp juniper berries

2 cardamom pods

2 allspice berries

1 cinnamon stick

2 sprigs fresh tarragon

2 tbsp olive oil

2 apples, peeled, cored, and diced

1 shallot, finely chopped

One 3-inch piece ginger, peeled
and finely chopped

4 cups chicken stock

2 cups heavy cream

1 cup apple cider
or juice from 2 apples

¼ cup apple brandy

¼ cup cider vinegar

¼ cup port or Madeira

Salt and pepper, to taste

Wrap the juniper berries, cardamom pods, allspice berries, cinnamon stick, and tarragon in a piece of cheesecloth, and tie with kitchen twine. Heat the oil in a large saucepan over medium-high heat. Add the apples, shallot, and ginger and sauté for 2 to 3 minutes, until the shallot starts to soften. Add the stock, cream, and apple juice or cider and stir, then add the spice bundle and bring to a brisk simmer. Lower the heat slightly and simmer until the liquid is reduced by half, about 30 to 40 minutes. Remove the cheesecloth bundle and purée the soup in batches in a blender . Return the soup to the saucepan and bring to a boil. Stir in the brandy, vinegar, and port or Madeira, and bring to a simmer. Season with salt and pepper to taste, and remove from heat.

SUSTAINABLE HARVESTING: THEN AND NOW

When settlers first arrived in Newfoundland, hunting migratory seabirds like the great auks and turrs (the local name for murres) was about survival. Swathes of rocky coastline, a short growing season, and a punishing climate made caring for cattle or working the land a constant struggle. Seabirds were readily available and chock-full of nutrients. Settlers weren't the first to value the seabirds, either. Archaeologists who unearthed a possible mortuary site in Port au Choix dating from around 2000 BCE found a burial suit of bones created from over 200 great auk skins. There's also plenty of evidence demonstrating that the Beothuk greatly valued the great auk and used the feathers, meat, and oils. Unfortunately for these birds, their eggs were a particularly sought-after prize; three times the size of a turr egg, each auk egg was filled with a giant, creamy yolk. They were easy prey for settlers—plentiful, and naively unafraid of hunters. Female auks only laid a single egg a year. The final nail in the great auk's coffin: they were too delicious. Their tender meat was highly prized and sought after by sailors, who eventually hunted them to extinction.

TURRS, RABBITS, AND OTHER GAME

The turr is a funny little bird; it waddles uncomfortably on land and looks as if it accidentally overdressed for a dinner party in black and white finery. The hunt for these little jokers has always been important here—it was even listed as a precondition when Joey Smallwood began negotiating for Newfoundland to enter Confederation. In fact, apart from Indigenous people, Newfoundlanders and Labradorians are the only people in North America allowed to pursue this particular hunt. Seabirds in most parts of the world are protected by treaties and acts.

Dr. Bill Montevecchi, professor of psychology, biology, and ocean sciences at Memorial University, is concerned about the disregard some hunters have. "There have been instances recently where it seems people are discarding turrs without using any part of the bird. It's not right."

Montevecchi isn't against the turr hunt, but believes that regulating and enforcing bag limits is essential to its survival. "The hunt looks a lot different than it used to. It used to be a skip and a musket. Now, there's automatic weapons. There's just not enough people on the water enforcing the hunt." The value for Montevecchi is in how the culture of the hunt enriches people's lives. "You see on turr Facebook groups folks who are bluntly disregarding the bag limit, but then you see others sharing recipes. You see people talking about their mouths watering, how excited they are to get their turr. That has value. There's no reason for that to stop if the hunt is regulated."

Seventeen-year-old Taylor Reid couldn't agree more. She's been going into the woods with her father from a young age. In the last year, she's finally been old enough to hunt and to carry a weapon herself. Reid's got her moose, skinned rabbits, and trapped coyotes; this is her second year getting turrs with her father. Hunting turrs is not for the faint of heart. The hunt involves an open boat on icy water, and the waves can be relentless. Reid explains: "It's freezing out there. The last time I went, I wore several pairs of pants, two hoodies, a survival suit, a sweat-wicking shirt, three pairs of socks, and heating pads tucked into my shoes."

Reid and her father went out to Placentia Bay and got their limit a few weeks ago. "We have a turr plucker, which saves us so much time. We use the feathers for bait; the head and tail get used as bait when we trap. We eat every part. Hearts and livers are our favourites—season them with salt and pepper, fry them with onions and butter. It's delicious." Reid says that the family treats the birds like chicken. "They go into the roaster with veggies. We also make duff that we use to scoop up the turr gravy—that's the best part." Reid and her family even use bones and skulls to create art. "Just yesterday, my dad and I spent the evening in the shed tie-dying skulls and painting them."

Becoming a wildlife officer is a dream of Reid's. She also does the local pageant circuit and writes essays about sustainable hunting as part of her pageant package. "I want to teach people about the importance of sustainable hunting. One, the meat of wild animals is healthy for us, but I think being outside is the most important part. If we spend time outside in the woods, we're more likely to take care for the woods." That's not to say Reid isn't aware of some of the unethical hunting happening around her. "Just a few weeks ago, a seal was out on the ice in our community. It was about 200 metres from land and you could see it from the playground. Some man drove up, rolled down his window, and shot the seal from his truck. The seal died slowly. That man could have hurt someone. He just drove away. That's the kind of thing I don't understand. That's disrespectful. It's pointless. He didn't eat the seal or use any part of it." Reid has also had some run-ins with the anti-sealing crowd. "My dad took me out on a sealing adventure when I was little. I posted a picture to the Facebook wall of a hunter I really admired. The photo was stolen by the anti-sealing crowd and photoshopped. Folks like that fuel me. I know humans have an important role in animal population control. In fact, I just finished my seal harvesting certificate."

Jennifer Shears is also no stranger to run-ins with the anti-sealing crowd. As a co-owner of the Natural Boutique on Water Street and a wildlife museum on the west coast of Newfoundland, Shears confronts protesters several times a year. "Blood on white snow is never going to look good. It's a stark image, but humans have been hunting seals for millennia. If we were to take ourselves out of the equation now, seals would get to the carrying capacity. Seals starving to death or being overtaken by disease isn't a prettier look." Shears points out that seal meat is organic and that clothing made from pelts is biodegradable; her priorities, when it comes to creating and sourcing products for her shop, are local and Indigenous. "Well, I'm a Mi'kmaw woman myself, and we've built a business model around small towns and supporting Indigenous hunters. Our tannery is in Dildo. We're carrying some new products from Nunavut. It's just a priority for us." Shears does not necessarily think that an anti-sealing stance is racist: "I think it's an ignorant perspective, and ignorance is a huge part of racism, but I think it has more to do with the power of marketing and the misconceptions around the hunt." Some of the common myths surrounding the industry include the idea that seals are endangered, babies are clubbed, and carcasses are wasted.

"If anything, the seal population is out of control. Babies aren't harvested, but the adult animals who have likely already reproduced are. Pelts are collected, meat is taken, and remaining parts are used on other trophic levels." Sheers is hopeful that the myths surrounding these traditional hunts are slowly being busted: "It just seems senseless that anti-hunters pretend we're not part of the ecosystem, that we're somehow separate from it. That's the kind of thinking that does the real harm."

BAKED TURR

Turr meat is dark and uncompromising, and the smell while it's cooking reminds me of a can of sardines packed in oil. It's like a more delicious and succulent duck. It's hard to come by, but sometimes I get lucky, and a hunter shares their harvest. Here's a traditional recipe for baked turr; you'll notice that a lot of important details are missing. Such is the mystery of old recipes.

Old-School Baked Turr
(Makes 12 to 14 buns)

4 cups flour
1/2 tsp baking soda
1/2 tsp baking powder
1 cup molasses
1 lb salt pork,
chopped and minced
water

Mince or chop pork and place in hot water to remove some of the salt. Let stand for five minutes. Sift dry ingredients. Remove pork from water and add to molasses. Add flour mixture to molasses mixture, alternatively with water to make a soft dough. Pat out on floured board and cut into pieces. Bake at 400F for 20 to 25 minutes.

Baked Turr 2.0

MAKES ENOUGH FOR 4 TO 6 PEOPLE

Okay, turr is TOUGH, so softening it up and infusing the bird with flavour with a brine is very important. My brine recipe is here too. I wanted to include some of the flavours that I like best with duck!

for the brine

2 dried chilies

2 tsp peppercorns

5 whole star anise

6 cups water

1 cup brown sugar

¾ cup salt

½ cup soy sauce

6 cloves garlic, smashed

3 knobs ginger, whole

for the turr

1 small onion, chopped

1 leek, chopped

½ cup roughly chopped parsnips

½ cup roughly chopped turnip

½ cup roughly chopped potatoes in large pieces

¼ cup olive oil

1 turr, brined

3 tbsp butter

3 tsp sea salt, and a little extra for tossing

1 tsp pepper

1 tsp savoury

to brine the turr

Toast the chilies, peppercorns, and star anise in a hot pot for about one minute. Add 3 cups of water to the pot along with brown sugar, salt, soy sauce, garlic cloves, and ginger. Bring to a boil. Stir to dissolve salt and sugar then remove from the heat. Add the remaining 3 cups of water, and wait until the brine is cool before pouring over your turr. I let my turr brine overnight.

to bake the turr

In the morning, I chopped up the onion, leek, parsnips, turnip, and potatoes. I tossed these in olive oil and sea salt and threw them into the bottom of the roasting pan. I took the turr out of the brine and patted it dry. Then I brushed butter onto the skin and seasoned it with salt, pepper, and savoury. I wanted the brine to infuse these cool flavours into the bird, but I wanted the actual roasting to be traditional. I set the oven for 375°F and roasted the turr for about an hour and a half.

TIP > You can add three cups of water to the bottom if you wish to make gravy, but I felt like it was delicious without. Fishy and duck-like, somehow!

Normally, I don't struggle with wine pairing, but turr stumped me. In the end, I had a beer.

A (VERY) BRIEF HISTORY OF CODFISH IN NEWFOUNDLAND

The cod fishery is another traditional hunt, but I'm not sure we could call the industry as a whole sustainable. The history of this hunt is lengthy and complicated, and it deserves (and has!) whole books devoted to it. I don't have that kind of space, so I'll jump to the inevitable disaster.

To summarize, the number of codfish off the Grand Banks, once considered an inexhaustible resource, dipped dangerously low in the 1990s. The federal government declared a moratorium on commercial cod fishing.

It's pretty difficult to pinpoint exactly what went wrong here, but it's not a stretch to say that the fishery was mismanaged, that fishing technology had improved, giving humans an unfair upper hand, and that the moratorium was declared too late. The unfortunate truth of this situation is that with warming waters, a full recovery of codfish stocks may never happen.

I've included a few cod recipes in this book; fresh cod recipes reside in the Spring and Summer section, but I tend to make cod cakes in the winter. They feel like a comfort food to me.

Though I do want you to try the recipes in the Book, I'd urge you to consume cod sustainably.

Buy from fishers directly. Shop at small sustainable seafood shops. Go handlining for your own cod when the food fishery opens.

Andie's Version of Old-School Salt Cod Cakes

MAKES ENOUGH FOR 4 PEOPLE

I never take the time to make salt cod cakes in the summer or fall. The produce in those seasons is so lush and bountiful that I forget all about salt cod. Cod cakes are a special winter treat.

1 ½ lbs salt cod

¼ cup butter

1 onion, chopped

6 cups potato, mashed

1 egg, beaten

½ tsp pepper

2 tbsp dried savoury (optional)

Canola oil for frying

1 cup scruncheons (optional)

Soak the salt cod in cold water overnight. To make the cod cakes, rinse the cod, then simmer in boiling water for about 15 minutes. Drain the water off the fish and allow the fish to cool to almost room temperature. When the fish is cool, flake it apart into small pieces with a fork. In a sauté pan, melt the butter over medium heat. Add the onions and cook until they are softened. Add the flaked fish along with the mashed potato, egg, pepper, and savoury. Mix together until well combined, then form into small cakes and roll in flour. Fry the fish cakes in canola oil over medium heat until golden brown on both sides. Serve with scruncheons if desired.

Cod Cakes with Sesame, Lime, and Miso

MAKES ENOUGH FOR 4 PEOPLE

I'm basing this dish on a little small plate I created in my restaurant days, which was a sake-miso-smoked-black-cod thing. That dish really only worked in theory, because the sake got absorbed and the flavour disappeared, but the miso comes through beautifully.

2 tbsp sesame oil, plus extra for greasing

2 fresh cod fillets, deboned

Salt and pepper

1 cup mashed potatoes

1 lime, zested and juiced

1 tbsp chopped green onion

1 tbsp white miso

½ cup flour

1 egg, beaten

½ cup breadcrumbs

This cod cake recipe uses fresh cod instead of salted.

First, we're going to cook it on the stovetop. Lightly coat the base of a non-stick pan with 1 tablespoon of the sesame oil, then place the pan over medium heat. Pat down the cod with paper towel and then season liberally with salt and pepper. Once the pan is hot, place the cod in the pan. Cook for about 3 minutes, until it's a nice golden colour. Carefully, turn the cod over and cook for 2 to 3 more minutes depending on how thick the fish is. Once it's cooked, flake the cod into a bowl and mix in the mashed potatoes, lime zest and juice, green onion, and miso paste.

Place flour, beaten egg, and breadcrumbs each in separate bowls. Divide the potato and cod mixture into eight cakes. Dust each patty with the flour, dip it in the egg, then coat it in breadcrumbs. Heat another tablespoon of sesame oil in a large frying pan over medium heat. Fry the patties for about 5 minutes on each side.

I like to serve this with a garlic aïoli, but some people will insist on mustard pickles.

HARVESTING CHAGA SUSTAINABLY

I really love foraging, but I'm not the expert. That would be Shawn Dawson of the Barking Kettle, or Lori McCarthy of Cod Sounds, or the good folks working at Nature NL. I'm more like a passionate enthusiast than an expert. There are a lot of reasons to love getting in the woods and hunting for ingredients. Stumbling upon a chanterelle patch is the most fun. It makes me feel like an old-timey prospector who finally struck it rich. I also consider an afternoon stirring wild berry jam or making a nettle pesto to be time well spent.

As far as trends go, foraging for wild ingredients is way healthier for our bodies and minds than feeding a Tamagotchi, planking, or calling a song a "bop" (a very specific pet peeve of mine). There's a downside, though. When a food becomes trendy via bloggers and foodies, there's a chance that that food will become over-harvested. That's happening with chaga right now.

For decades—perhaps longer—chaga has been a traditional medicine in Russia and other northern regions. Chaga has long been important to different Indigenous groups in Canada, so sustainable harvesting should be of the utmost importance. Herbalists often recommend chaga for a whole variety of ailments. While not all of the claims surrounding chaga can be substantiated, chaga is certainly rich in antioxidants and it can be flavourful if you take the time to play with it. It's also very popular right now. Blog after blog will give you step-by-step instructions on how to make chaga teas, powders, and coffees. Influencers and celebrities sip it every morning. You can even purchase tinctures of it on "wellness" websites on the internet. Newfoundland is rife with it, but not everyone is harvesting this fungus in a safe or sustainable way. On a recent trip to the Central region, I noticed that people were hacking into birch trees, leaving no trace of the chaga, and cutting directly into the tree.

Although technically not a mushroom, chaga is often given the title "king of the mushrooms."

This king is a fungus that grows on the bark of birch trees in cold climates. To me, they look like big black bumpy ears. I met up with Shawn Dawson, forager and owner of the Barking Kettle, to learn how to safely and sustainably harvest chaga.

1 Identify correctly.

Chaga tends to form domes and odd horns on birch trees. It's not usually a symmetrical growth. It's black and crusty-looking, but the real tell is the golden interior. It gleams likes fool's gold. The most common look-alike is a burl. Burls are outward growths that tend to be symmetrical. They can be caused by physical trauma to the tree, insects, or other fungal growths.

2 Harvest at the right time and in the right place.

"Well, first, make sure the tree is alive" is Shawn's most important piece of advice for us. Chaga is a parasite of the birch tree. The relationship is truly symbiotic. When the tree dies, so does the fungus. Obviously, we don't want to be eating dead rotting chaga, so Shawn recommends looking for winter buds, to make sure the tree is alive. Similarly, chaga tends to act like a big sponge and absorbs pollutants in the air: "Best to go deep in the woods and leave the chaga on the side of the highway alone." Finally, Shawn harvests chaga in the late fall and winter. The sap isn't running yet, so the chaga is more likely to be dry.

3 Harvest carefully.

Chaga usually grows somewhat high up in trees. Shawn always climbs the tree carefully, and he doesn't wear spikes, to prevent damage to the tree. "Chaga can take forty years to grow, so taking the whole piece doesn't make sense. It's important that people leave at least a third. It'll grow back faster, and it's just more sustainable." He also points out that you never want to slice into the tree. Slice into the chaga instead.

4 Dry it. Freeze it. Get creative with it.

Chaga can get mouldy quickly, but it freezes well! If you can't clean and dry it quickly, then freeze it until you're ready to tackle the chore. If you have the time, make sure you begin by dusting the chaga with a mushroom brush. There's going to be some forest debris on it that you might not want to ingest. Cut the chaga into two-inch chunks. This part might be tricky, so use a sharp knife. You can dry chaga at room temperature, or speed up the process by dehydrating it in your oven overnight. Shawn turns his dehydrated chaga chunks into powder using his coffee grinder.

I followed Shawn's instructions and made chaga tea, but I wanted some more ideas. Shawn often pairs it with chocolate, as the fullness of the chocolate rounds out the chaga. He also loves it with other woody, rounded flavours and mentioned that the Newfoundland Distillery has been making an award-winning chaga rum, while the Mill Street Brewery uses chaga in a stout. Play with it!

5 Try chaga before harvesting!

It would be a shame if you found the flavour repulsive and tossed your chaga harvest into the trash. If you want to try chaga but aren't sure if you'll like the flavour, try some of the Barking Kettle's products (available at the St. John's Farmers' Market) before taking a piece of chaga off a tree.

6 Only take what you need!

If you do like the flavour and want the experience of harvesting, make sure you only take what you need. "A little chaga goes a long way," says Dawson. "A piece the size of a grapefruit will see most people through a winter." Trends come and go, but chaga is a finite resource that we need to protect; the best way to do that is to harvest it sustainably.

Chaga Tea Recipe

MAKES ABOUT 6 TO 8 CUPS OF TEA

4 individual chunks dried chaga, each about 1 inch long

4 cups water

½ tsp vanilla extract

Select 4 pieces of chaga and add these to a pot filled with 4 cups of water. Add vanilla extract. Slowly bring the pot to a simmer and keep it there a minimum of 15 minutes. Strain the chaga chunks from the tea, and serve the tea hot, immediately. I usually take the time to sweeten my chaga tea with honey and maple syrup.

A QUICK SIDE JOURNEY TO RUG HOOKING

As I mentioned earlier, late winter and early spring are tough in Newfoundland. Desserts, homemade bread, warm drinks, good books, and crafts are how I struggle through until the crocuses pop up. A little write-up on the history of crafts might not seem like a natural thing to include in a cookbook, but food history is entwined with crafting history; they both have to do with the traditions of hearth and home. More specifically, the history of crafts, such as knitting and rug hooking, is not well recorded, and food history is hard to trace, too. Oh, you can find all kinds of handwritten recipes, but actually finding someone's recorded experience is virtually impossible. Crafts and kitchen work often belonged to women and folks who lived on the lower end of the socio-economic scale—two groups whose experiences were rarely recorded or considered important.

I fell in love with rug hooking during the early days of the pandemic, but it's been my favourite craft for as long as I can remember. I've always tried to take in exhibitions and openings that feature textile artists, and I've long had the habit of strolling through the fabric store, touching all the soft and expensive yarns wistfully. (Remember when we could touch everything without fear of infection? Good times.)

Like many of us in the pre-COVID-19 world, I was too busy rushing from one meeting to the next to find the time to learn something new. I sit on boards, do freelance writing, and owned a small catering business. I take on part-time contracts with different non-profit organizations. In March, when my business closed and everyone began hoarding toilet paper and buying large amounts of Lysol, I ordered two beginner rug kits from a local Newfoundland maker. Within a week, I was hooked (pardon the pun).

Rug hooking is an art form in which rugs or wall hangings are made by pulling yarn or fabric through a stiff woven base, and it's a craft that came to Newfoundland through the economics of poverty.

More specifically, European floor coverings of the 1800s were expensive, and only the richest merchant settlers and shipbuilders of St. John's could send away for them. The rest of those early colonists, with the wolf at their door and the cold creeping in, made do by weaving household rags or scraps of fabric together to make the rugs they could not afford to buy.

Winnie Glavine, the social media director of the Rug Hooking Guild of Newfoundland and Labrador, and owner of Hooked Creations NL, maintains that rug hooking wasn't taught at the finishing schools in St. John's. Instead, evidence suggests rug hooking was a bayman's craft. "Oh, the finishing schools taught ladies how to set a table and how to embroider, but if someone in St. John's wanted a rug, they either asked a bayman to make it or they sent away for one."

Rug hooking has a long tradition in Newfoundland and can be traced back to the seventeenth century. While it seems to have come from England and Ireland, its exact origins as a craft are difficult to trace. The Rug Hooking Guild of Newfoundland and Labrador has some examples of mats that are over a hundred years old. Glavine describes their heritage, saying, "These mats were made to be used; they weren't hangings for the wall. They were trod on and placed in front of the fire. It really shows us just how these mats were made to last." Some of the popular patterns were simple blocks, flags, or Bible verses. Folks also made what they saw in their backyards. There are many examples of rugs featuring fishing boats, whales, or bright saltbox houses.

"Another thing that happened frequently is that someone from the community would leave the island to work on the mainland and bring back a pattern from a city that would then get shared amongst the women in the community. Each woman might make the pattern a little differently, putting their own spin on it. The *Sidewalks of New York* pattern is a great example of this," says Glavine.

Glavine tried to convince her grandmother to teach her the art form in the 1970s, but by that time rug hooking had gone out of fashion and was in danger of fading away. Her grandmother refused to teach her: "That's work. You don't want to learn that."

Finally, Glavine learned how to rug hook from a rug-hooking workshop in the early 1990s. She joined the Guild shortly afterwards. "We've very much tried to take the craft into modern times." This means lots of folks today are using quality yarn instead of household scraps. Many artists are hand-dyeing their wool with natural botanicals. The mats of yesteryear have evolved into wall hangings, mittens, pillows, and floor coverings. Some artists mix their textile arts, using other techniques combined with rug hooking.

One of my favourite local artists is Molly White. She's the one who sold me the starter rug hooking kits I mentioned, through her store Molly Made, located in Woody Point. For White, "rug hooking is very much a living art form." She mixes her rugs with other textile arts, fabrics, and even found objects. Although her methods are not traditional, White prefers to use pantyhose instead of yarn or scrap fabrics, because she believes it creates a finer line. She also experiments with texture. "Actually, there's a huge difference between what I produce commercially and what I produce creatively. For my kits, I draw what people see in Newfoundland, familiar scenes, but for myself, I like to comb the shores and incorporate shells and driftwood into my pieces."

Glavine and White both work full-time as artists—teaching, designing kits, and producing commercial pieces. They are also both huge promoters of other artists in their community. White was quick to sing the praises of Deanne Fitzpatrick. "She's originally from Placentia, and her style is inspiring and bright." Meanwhile, Glavine mentioned Joan Foster (one of the founding members of the Guild) as both an outstanding artist and a person who has striven to preserve the history of rug hooking in Newfoundland and Labrador.

So, what if you're interested in rug hooking but you don't feel like an artist in any way? At this, Glavine piped up, "You don't need to draw! If you want to do your own patterns then you just need to be able to draw basic outlines of shape." I'm planning to stick with my new rug-hooking hobby, and I asked both ladies what rug hooking has brought to their lives. They gave curiously similar answers. For White, "The biggest gift it's given me is a sense of soothing and calm." "Folks always say, 'You must need some patience for that,'" says Glavine, "and I tell them, 'No. Rug hooking gives me patience. It helps me have patience.'"

Mid-Spring
to Summer

Spring in Newfoundland happens late and happens so quickly that I've jammed it in with summer—it's when foraging, fishing, and farming really get underway. It's also the time of year when hobby gardeners (such as myself) plot our gardens and start our seeds. Basically, Newfoundland's long, slow spring is a season of anticipation. Although I try my best to make winter fun and enjoy all that the season has to offer, I start wishing and waiting for signs of spring as early as March, which is a pretty foolhardy thing to do in Newfoundland. This past year, with the pandemic and all the related uncertainty, I really channelled my energy and anxiety into planting and starting

seeds, so I'm including some information on that here. Growing food and eating it go together, so where better than a cookbook to combine that knowledge?

GROWING

I grew up on a homestead, and my folks now own a small beef farm. My mom is also a world-class gardener and owns her own landscaping company. And yet I still felt uncertain and shy about growing vegetables indoors. If I can be intimidated after that childhood, then it must seem overwhelming to others without that experience. So I consulted with my friend Sarah (a horticulturist and expert) on starting seeds indoors and had an amazing harvest this past year.

STARTING SEEDS

Starting seeds indoors can seem like a monumental task if you've never attempted it before. Here are my tips. First, gather your supplies. You'll need the following things: seeds, cell trays, pots (you can save money by using egg cartons or cardboard berry containers; just make sure you poke some drainage holes in the bottom), a light, a spray bottle full of water, a table or cart to place your trays on, a fan, and some good soil. Lots of folks will assert that you don't need to buy any fancy indoor lighting equipment to start seeds, you just need to have a nice consistent bright light. Well, I live in an old downtown row house and I haven't seen a full day of consistent bright sunshine in some time, so I bought a four-foot-long full-spectrum fluorescent light and jury-rigged it to hang from the ceiling. It doesn't seem to use too much electricity, doesn't create too much heat, and was reasonably priced—which felt very important, since I was without work for the first few months of the pandemic. Sarah suggested placing the lights about an inch above my trays. As the little shoots emerge, the light gets raised to allow room for growth. If you do opt to start seeds without a light, just know that your seeds may stretch and become weakened, so give them their best shot by placing them in the most sunlit spot in your house.

Once your seedlings begin poking through the soil, they will start to straighten up and unfurl, and this is when you'll move the little guys under a light source. Your seeds don't need light right away, but they do need labels! I can't tell you how many times I've planted seeds and have had to wait months to figure out what I've grown.

There's a lot to say on the topic of seeds. Sarah wisely cautioned against starting too much too soon, saying, "People tend to overdo it, get overwhelmed, and then give up on gardening as a hobby. Start small and grow things you'll actually eat." For me, that means tons of greens, herbs, tomato seeds, kale (I'm an addict), and chamomile for tea (I drink buckets of the stuff). It's important to keep in mind that if you're planning on gardening indoors, then all of your seeds will need to be transplanted into larger pots that will take up way more space. If you're going to transplant these seeds to an outdoor plot, you'll need to harden off the seeds— I'll explain more about that below. Once you get more comfortable with gardening, you can expand and grow other things. Sarah grows pineapples, olives, lemons, and avocados—all indoors!

Seeds are fairly affordable, so try a variety. Sowing the seeds is the easy part! Just place a few seeds on the surface of the seed-starting mix and then gently press them down! Some seeds, like thyme, can be left entirely uncovered. Other seeds will require more darkness to germinate, so read your seed packets carefully.

I plant about three seeds per individual cell. Because some of the seeds won't germinate; if they do, you can thin them out later.

I grew up in a house that went through bags and bags of peat moss each spring. To be honest, I never spared a thought for the sustainability of that soil—I just thought it was what gardeners used. "Peat moss is actually not a renewable resource. The bogs that it comes from in Europe releases massive amount of CO_2 when peat is harvested, and it causes damage to these wetlands." Sarah suggested that I buy coco coir soil instead. "It's a more sustainable potting mix

that combines a by-product of coconuts with soil. It works really wonderfully, and I just feel better about using it."

You'll want to fill the seed trays two-thirds full. Lightly shake the trays so that the potting mix can settle. Don't pack it down; you want the soil to be aerated. Also, I've been known to baby my plants to death via overwatering. Sarah pointed out that I need to ditch the watering can: "Seeds want to be lightly misted, so a spray bottle is your best method." My other big mistake is that I feel the soil to see if it's dry; once it's dry to the touch, I water my seedling. Sarah confirmed that this is a big no-no. "Yeah, don't do that. Judge by weight instead. Pick up your trays just before you water them. Pick them up after you've watered them. Feel the difference. Once your trays are light again, then it's time for another misting."

New seedlings are susceptible to damping off. That's a gardening term for a fungus that enters seedlings via the soil and kills them. Luckily, you can prevent this by placing a fan near the seedlings. Don't set it on high—we're not looking to create Wreckhouse winds, just a gentle breeze—and leave it on during the day.

And that's my guide to starting seeds.

SOIL TIPS

Okay, now we need to talk soil for raised beds. Some people don't care for them, but there are so many reasons to use raised beds. For one, the soil in Newfoundland is littered with rocks. Moreover, the ground in many cities is contaminated with lead and yard pesticides and other nasty things that have leached beneath the surface. Raised beds combat this and also deter pests. Stooping is minimized, and most importantly, you get to select the type of soil you use. Raised beds equals total control of soil quality.

There are usually four types of soil you can buy from a garden centre:

GARDEN SOIL Think of this as enriched all-purpose flour. This soil will work well in most raised gardens. It contains additives like fertilizer or other plant foods, which will help things sprout nicely. Just be careful to check the soil composition because some types contain synthetic fertilizers—good for flowers, but not carrots. Remember: anything in your dirt ends up in your food, so read the label!

TOPSOIL It's all in the name. Topsoil is literally soil that has been scraped from the top of the ground. Topsoil usually doesn't contain additives, so you have to feed it. I consider this to be a great base. I usually buy a few bags of topsoil, then mix in kelp and compost.

POTTING SOIL Lighter and looser than garden soil, it also contains little white balls throughout the bag. This is called "perlite" or "vermiculite." These are additives that help aerate the soil, help retain nutrients, and hold moisture. I like to grab a bag of potting soil for my containers and planters.

TRIPLE MIX For a long time, this stuff was considered the gold star of vegetable gardens. Triple mix usually includes topsoil, peat moss, and compost or manure. The peat moss helps to lock in moisture, and the manure feeds the soil and increases plant growth. I used to use triple mix, but peat moss is not a sustainable resource, so I don't buy it anymore.

Now we need to talk about feeding and caring for your soil. When you garden in the same space and same soil each year, the plants suck up nutrients. Eventually, if you don't feed your soil, your vegetables will lack flavour and nutrition. Soil isn't a dry, dead thing. It's teeming with life: worms, bugs, microbes, and even fungi. These helpers release nutrients into the soil when they decompose organic matter. They burrow, creating networks of tunnels, and when they move, their pathways aerate and loosen the soil. When you feed your soil, you're keeping all the biodiversity in your dirt alive and well.

One of the essential ingredients for healthy soil is compost, which just means decaying organic materials. Sometimes people confuse compost with fertilizer, but there's an important distinction. Fertilizers feed the plants, while compost actually feeds and enriches the soil. If you have a nice big yard, picking a corner to build a compost pile is a great idea, but you can compost in a small space, too. Composting has become trendy, which means there are surprisingly stylish composters available for purchase that will look great in your small yard. Simply follow the instructions and you'll have compost in no time.

For those building a compost pile, here's what goes in the mix:

> **Ashes:** Firepit or woodstove ashes contain lime! This helps balance the pH of your compost.

> **Eggshells:** There is so much calcium in eggshells. Crunch them up and let them decay, but don't worry if you can still see them.

> **Coffee grounds:** Old grounds add acidity to the compost.

> **Leaves:** Unlike most people, I get frustrated when neighbours rake their leaves and then bag them up. That's free organic decay! Leaves are great for your soil, so if you can't stand them in your yard, dump them on your compost pile.

> **Food scraps:** Apple peels and cores, carrot peels—basically any vegetable matter adds nutrients to your compost.

> **Hair:** Okay, admittedly this seems gross, but hair (both human and pet) is rich in nitrogen. Lots of folks put hair in their compost piles and see excellent results.

> **Manure:** Manure contains so many nutrients for plants. There's a lot to dig into here—whole books have been written on manure, so I'm just going to cover some basics. I personally like to buy bagged manure from a garden centre because it's often sterilized. E-coli poisoning is not a good look. There's nothing wrong with using raw manure, though! In time, it will enrich the soil and help it teem with life. You can buy manure from farmers. Here's a pro tip: look to the back of the pile, where the oldest manure lives. If you do buy raw manure, make sure it sits in your compost pile for at least a year before you use it. Sometimes folks will put dog or cat waste into manure piles, but that's a hard NO for compost you plan to grow vegetables with (it's swarming with pathogens). You could put it into compost for flower beds, though.

> **Worms:** If you'd rather not dig them up, head to a fishing supply store. These little animals are crucial to a healthy compost pile.

If you're planning to make your own compost heap, remember to turn it over now and then with a shovel. Also, keep your dog away from the heap. My hound has rolled around in compost and it's a special kind of nightmare I wouldn't wish on anyone. When it comes to mixing compost into your soil, you don't need to get too scientific. Make sure the pile contains all the right ingredients, let it age, and then mix the compost into your bed as you see fit. You really can't use too much compost! Toss it around with your topsoil. Then follow these next steps.

Consider adding kelp and seaweed to your garden. Newfoundlanders have been using seaweed on their gardens for centuries. I recently added kelp to my gardening bed after a neighbour picked some up for me. I spread it on my plot and now I'm letting all the goodness leak into the topsoil. I've been advised to let it sit on top of my soil for a week or two, and then mix and distribute it throughout. Some folks dry it out over the summer and then use it the following spring. Kelp adds selenium, which doesn't occur naturally in Newfoundland dirt, to the soil. If you trek out to a beach to grab kelp for your beds, make sure the beach is clean; you're allowed to remove kelp, but try not to disturb the local ecosystem any more than you have to. Please don't trek into the water and pull it out!

Finally, you'll want to buy some fertilizer. Before you do, invest in a soil-testing kit, or send a sample of your soil to the Department of Fisheries, Forestry and Agriculture.

Soil testing is important because different areas lack different nutrients, and fertilizer that works for one garden might not suit others.

You don't want to add too much nitrogen, for example, and you won't know how much you need before testing your soil. If you're unsure about how to read or understand your soil test results, take them in to one of the local garden centres. There, they'll interpret the results and let you know what kind of fertilizer you'll need.

That's it! Compost, kelp, some good bagged soil from one of the local garden centres, and a little fertilizer will help maintain good soil health in your raised beds.

FORAGING

Those last few snowstorms never feel cozy like the others; instead, they feel like a betrayal. When the snow finally melts and I can forage, I get so excited. Wild food is a part of this place. Dandelion has long been picked for its liver-cleansing properties, spruce tips were used to fight off scurvy, and berry picking has always been an important as a source of food. Having said that, lots of plants were left in the ground to rot, their edible properties ignored and left untested. Because of this, my recipes for foraged foods do vary from the standard formula that I've followed for most of the book! Instead of posting an old recipe and my new take on it, sometimes we'll just have to make do with a singular newish recipe. Also, most of my foraging recipes are for small amounts. I'd rather you start small and see if you enjoy the flavour, rather than harvest large amounts of something you won't use. If you do enjoy them, each recipe can be doubled or tripled with ease! Here's a simple, but effective list of dos and don'ts to use as a guideline if you're new to foraging.

Becoming an expert in mushroom picking takes years and years. I've been hunting for a long time, and even I don't really go outside the comfort zone of chanterelles, hedgehogs, and the occasional bolete. Don't start your foraging adventure with mushrooms! Start with spring greens and summer berries. They are easily identifiable! Nettles, dandelions, sorrel, and other spring greens are easy to find, easy to cook with, and most likely won't hurt you. Learn about wild food slowly. There's no need to rush this!

Here are some good rules to follow:

IMPORTANT: *Don't eat what you don't recognize!*
Look, I've popped grass into my mouth a dozen times, thinking it was sorrel. Don't do this. Grass isn't great-tasting, but there are more dangerous things than that to accidentally put in your mouth. Give yourself lots of time to really practice your identifying skills.

Seek out an expert.
There are loads of knowledgeable people here in Newfoundland. Foray Newfoundland hosts a number of workshops on mushroom foraging; the Memorial University Botanical Gardens has a variety of resources on gardening, composting, and other related areas; and there are foragers at the Farmers' Market in St. John's who would be happy to answer your questions.

Don't focus solely on the woods.
There's probably an invasive species or two in your own yard! Japanese knotweed, dandelions, goutweed, and stinging nettles are all delicious, and you don't have to look far to find them.

Don't take too much!
It's easy to clear out a chanterelle patch or to pick every last blackberry from the bramble, but remember that animals often rely on these seasonal treats. Take only what you need.

Check your surroundings.
Picking spring greens from Bannerman Park is not a good idea. There are so many pups and people walking everywhere, vehicle exhaust, and other litter. City foraging, in general, is just not a solid plan! Similarly, consider how close you are to a highway; certain wild foods like chaga act as environmental filters and absorb all kinds of things. Foraging is fun and exciting, but make sure you're confident about the quality of what you're picking.

Nuisance weeds are tasty, and cooking and eating them can be a very satisfying revenge!

Stinging Nettle Pesto

MAKES ENOUGH TO FILL 1 SMALL MASON JAR

Stinging nettles are a wild plant that you can eat with vengeance in your heart. Nettles have been used as a herbal remedy for thousands of years. Although actual reports of their health benefits vary widely from study to study, many people believe that nettles can help with circulation, allergies, and prostate issues. I'm not a doctor and cannot verify any of those claims. As a chef, I can confirm that nettles are incredibly delicious, and you can make some-thing with them very quickly! I catered a wedding a few years ago and just outside the kitchen there was a massive patch of nettles. During my prep time, I became increasingly worried that someone would have a few too many and fall into the patch. I decided to throw on gloves and pick most of the patch. Twenty minutes later, I had a bowl of nettle pesto bottled and in the fridge! Once the chaotic wedding catering was wrapped, I had a little treat to take home with me.

There are rules for working with nettles. First, you have to blanch your nettles before you process them, or they will sting you, and you will be grumpy. Also, blanching locks the colour in beautifully. I have skipped this step before, and the result is a very unappetizing brown pesto. To blanch nettles, get a huge pot of water boiling and add a handful of salt. Grab the nettles with gloved hands and put them into the boiling water. Stir around and boil for about 90 seconds. Fish them out with a skimmer or the tongs and immediately dump them into a big bowl with ice water in it. Once they are cool, put them in a colander to strain. Grab a tea towel and put the nettles in it. Wrap one end of the towel one way, then the other end of the towel the other way, and squeeze out as much moisture as you can. Chop them fine before making the pesto.

2 tbsp toasted
sunflower seeds

4 cloves garlic,
roughly chopped

2 heaping tbsp
grated Parmesan

1 cup blanched,
chopped nettles

Salt, to taste

¾ cup olive oil,
or more if you like
a runny pesto

Toast the sunflower seeds until golden brown. Next, pulse them in your food processor a few times. **NOTE: *Don't overdo this; you're making pesto, not sunflower-seed butter!*** Toss the garlic into the food processor. Add the Parmesan, blanched nettles, and salt.

Run the food processor so everything combines but isn't a smooth paste. You want it with some texture. Add the olive oil next. This part isn't an exact science; some folks like a thin pesto, others want it heavy, so add more or less to suit your own taste. I like to add a tablespoon at a time and let it incorporate fully before adding more.

I usually just spread nettle pesto on bread, but it's excellent stirred into soups. I also find that it complements beef well, and my husband likes it with pasta!

Wild Nettle Soup

MAKES ENOUGH FOR 4 TO 6 PEOPLE

Okay, two nettle recipes might seem excessive, but nettle soup is so tasty, so green, and so good for you that I just couldn't leave it out. You can serve this with a little yoghurt or sour cream, and a little nettle pesto drizzled over the top. Some feta crumbled on top would also be amazing.

1 bulb garlic

1 tsp canola oil

Pinch sea salt

2 tbsp butter

3 large green onions, chopped

2 tbsp flour

3 cups vegetable stock

3 cups fresh nettles, packed tightly

½ cup whipping cream

Salt and pepper, to taste

yoghurt, chilies, croutons, tarragon, lemon juice (optional, for garnish)

Toss a garlic bulb in a teaspoon of canola oil, sprinkle with sea salt, and roast in oven at 375°F for 30 minutes. Once it's roasted, press out four cloves and store the remaining roasted garlic for later use in other recipes.

Melt the butter in a large saucepan over a low-medium heat. Add the green onions, lower the heat a bit more, and cook until the onions have released their fragrance, about a minute or two. Sprinkle flour into the pan so that it coats everything. Next, gradually add the stock and whisk. Raise the heat to a boil and add the blanched nettles. Lower the heat and simmer for 2 to 3 minutes. **NOTE:** *Do not boil the nettles!*

Working in batches, purée the soup in a blender, adding the roasted garlic as you go. Return purée to the pot and stir in the cream. Season with salt and pepper.

Garnish with yoghurt, bird's eye chilies, croutons, tarragon, or anything you want. Potatoes or carrots can be added to thicken the soup and give it more body. A little squeeze of lemon can also brighten this up, but that's optional.

TIP > You can substitute coconut milk for the cream to make it vegan.

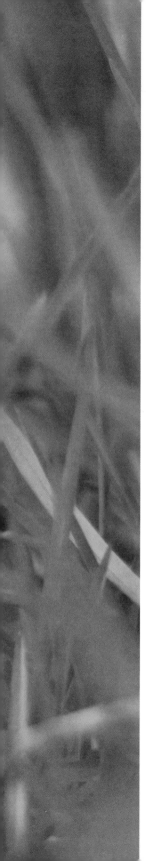

DANDELIONS

These were harvested by the earliest settlers in Newfoundland and were poetically called "Piss-a-Beds." They are a natural diuretic—hence their name—but their flavour is sharp! Like a more intense arugula, this is a sturdy green with some bite. I like it with garlic and lemon.

Dandelion greens are good steamed, as in the recipe I found in the *1973 Newfoundland Cook Book*, but better sautéed. You can also mix your dandelion greens with baby kale, edible flowers, and a little rich goat cheese to mellow the salad. Dandelion greens can technically be eaten throughout the summer but are best enjoyed in early spring. They tend to get tougher, stringier, and more bitter as the season progresses.

Steamed Dandelion Greens

Cut off ends, allowing the leaves to separate. Wash by placing greens in a pan of water and lifting out of water. Wash in several waters to remove any dirt. Cook in a large amount of water if you wish to remove the bitter flavor, or if the dandelions are old, they can be blanched in boiling water for five minutes, drained and covered with fresh water. Cook greens until tender usually 10-20 minutes. Chop greens before serving and season with butter, salt, and pepper. Pick dandelions, if possible, before they bloom to avoid bitterness.

New-School Dandelion Greens

MAKES ENOUGH FOR 2 TO 4 PEOPLE, AS A SIDE DISH

2 cups dandelion greens

1 tsp olive oil

¼ tsp red pepper flakes

Salt and pepper, to taste

1 clove garlic, minced

1 tsp lemon juice

Wash the dandelion greens and chop into medium pieces. Using a good cast-iron pan, heat the oil over medium heat. Toss in your greens, season with red pepper flakes, salt, and pepper. Cook for 2 to 3 minutes. Toss in garlic and a squeeze of lemon at the last possible minute. Remove from heat.

Dandelion Root "Coffee"

MAKES ENOUGH FOR 4 CUPS OF "COFFEE"

This recipe is a real pain in the butt. Pulling up the root of the dandelion is virtually impossible. You'll need a shovel. Also, cleaning the root is very challenging. I usually make this once in the spring. It's a fun experiment, but it's not in my weekly spring repertoire—too time-consuming! I've included it more for the sake of curiosity than anything else.

2 tbsp cleaned and chopped dandelion roots

1 tsp cinnamon

½ tsp ground cardamom

2 cups water

HAVE FUN! You can play around with this recipe and add whole spices instead. I've tried it with star anise too.

To roast the dandelion root
Preheat oven to 400°F. Start by scrubbing the roots well. You can soak the roots in buckets of cold water overnight, but attacking with vigour and a clean mushroom brush will work well too. Dry the roots and cut into half-inch long pieces. There will be little scrubby bits of roots; toss those. We just want the good, thick slices. Now, roast the dandelion roots for 30 minutes until they're dry and browned. **NOTE:** *Keep a close eye because these can burn quickly.*

To make the "coffee"
Place 2 tablespoons of the roasted dandelion root in a pot along with the ground spices. Add 2 cups of water and bring to a boil. Turn down heat and let it simmer for about 10 minutes. Strain using a fine mesh strainer. Sit back and enjoy with a little maple syrup for sweetness.

Dandelion Green Salad

MAKES ENOUGH FOR 4 PEOPLE, AS A SIDE SALAD

3 cups mixed greens

1 cup dandelion greens

¾ cup goat cheese

½ cup pickled rhubarb

¼ cup almonds, toasted

Small handful pansy petals, for colour (optional)

Simply toss all the ingredients together to make a beautiful spring salad.

Sometimes I'll dress this with a simple lemon vinaigrette—garlic, oil, lemon juice, salt, and pepper, with some Dijon if you feel like it. Other times, I find that I want something creamy to cut through the bitter greens and the sharpness of the pickled rhubarb. That's when I use the Dill and Sorrel Dressing on page 93.

Dill and Sorrel Dressing

MAKES ENOUGH TO FILL 1 LARGE MASON JAR

In Newfoundland, there are three different types of edible sorrels: garden sorrel, sheep sorrel, and curled dock. Sheep sorrel, more commonly known as "Sally Suckers," is my favourite type. It has a lemony astringent flavour that just works beautifully in soups and dressings. It's easy to identify too. The leaves are tinged red and are shaped like arrows. You can add more herbs or swap out the dill in this recipe. I often throw parsley into the mix.

2 ½ cups wild sorrel leaves

1 cup dill, finely chopped

1 ¼ cups plain skyr-type yoghurt

½ cup buttermilk

1 tbsp capers

1 tsp lemon juice

Salt, to taste

Wash the sorrel thoroughly and dry in a clean tea towel. Remove from towel and roll into a tight wad, then slice it as thinly as possible into a chiffonade. Blend all ingredients together in a food processor.

TIP > This dressing can be thinned with water if it's too thick for your liking.

It's delicious when served with lamb or fish.

Garlic Oil **MAKES 1 CUP**

Garlic oil is a must-have for the summer! I drizzle it onto salads! I brush it onto bread! I end up carting it on long fishing trips to pair with the bread recipe on page 94. It's always worth it.

1 bulb garlic

1 cup olive oil

1 tsp dill seed, toasted (optional)

Start by peeling the cloves out of the head of garlic and smashing them. Set aside. Heat the cup of olive oil at medium-low heat for 3 minutes. Toss in garlic and dill seeds and let it all cook together for about 4 minutes. Remove from heat. Let stand for an hour before using. Garlic oil goes with trout, chanterelles, steak, sautéed kale, and pretty much any vegetable.

My Only Spring and Summer Bread

MAKES ENOUGH FOR 6 TO 8 PEOPLE

From mid-spring until mid-summer, I'm barely baking at all. Instead, I spend my free time exploring the East Coast Trail, dragging my seedlings outside to harden off, and having cook-ups at the beach. This recipe is pretty much the extent of my summer baking. It's my favourite recipe for beach bread.

4 cups all-purpose flour

2 tsp fine sea salt

1 tsp instant dry yeast

1 tbsp olive oil

1 ⅓ cups warm water

Garlic oil for cooking (see recipe on page 93)

Put the flour in a bowl with salt and yeast. Add oil and warm water. Using a wooden spoon, mix all the ingredients until they loosely come together. Flour your hands a little. Turn the whole thing onto a floured surface and knead for 10 minutes until perfectly smooth. **NOTE:** *This is an absurdly loose dough, so don't sweat it if it seems too sticky; there's no need to add more flour.*

Oil a bowl, place the dough inside, and let it rise until it has doubled in size—about 2 hours. Punch the dough down, then divide into balls that are a little smaller than your fist. Now roll out these dough balls into little circles.

I place a sheet of parchment paper between each round of dough, then I wrap the whole thing in a clean kitchen towel and stick it in my cooler or picnic basket. When I get to the beach for my cook-out, I heat a cast-iron pan until it's smoking and then pour about a tablespoon of garlic oil into the pan. I lay one flatbread in the pan for about 2 minutes, flip it, then cook the other side for about 2 minutes as well. Then I remove it immediately from the pan and serve with a touch more garlicky oil, fried trout, smoked herring, or sautéed wild mushrooms. If you don't want to make these flatbreads at the beach, you can cook them at home in a frying pan. They freeze beautifully, too!

Knotweed Jam

MAKES ENOUGH TO FILL 1 LARGE MASON JAR

Hoo boy, this is an evil plant. Japanese knotweed is the most relentless of invasive species. You can burn it and douse it with chemicals, and its little greeny-red shoots just keep poking back up through the earth. The good news about Japanese knotweed, however, is that you can EAT it, which is excellent revenge for devaluing your property. Knotweed needs to be enjoyed in spring; otherwise, it's too woody and won't boil down. It gets bitter and harsh after it's about six inches tall, so try to harvest the early shoots when they are fresh out of the ground! I don't want to give you an official recipe here because knotweed behaves a little differently every time I use it. More specifically, some stalks are more watery and bitter than others, so tasting as you go is essential. Here's a rough guide to making knotweed jam.

GET AHEAD! The first thing is to gather young stalks of knotweed, wash them well and remove all twigs, leaves, and woody tips.

5 cups knotweed, chopped into 1-inch pieces

1 cup sugar

Lemon juice, to taste

Water

Rhubarb or beet juice for colour

Put the knotweed into a saucepan and add 1 cup of sugar for every 5 cups of stems—basically, treat the knotweed like rhubarb. Let your stems sit in the sugar on low heat for about 20 minutes. Add a little water if necessary, and stir occasionally. I add lemon juice and a little rhubarb or beet juice at this stage.

NOTE: *Knotweed cooks down into a brownish purée that is not incredibly appealing to look at. Rhubarb and beet juice won't alter the flavour but will make the whole jam prettier.*

When the jam is cooked and cooled, store in the fridge for up to three weeks.

I like knotweed jam on a cheese plate. It pairs well with an oozy brie and a hearty cracker.

Labrador Tea

MAKES ENOUGH TEA FOR 1 TEAPOT

I think that Labrador tea is one of the coolest plants. The flavour is piney and resiny, but still appealing. Identifying the plant is easy. The top of the leaf is dark green and has a leathery texture. The bottom side of each leaf is a rusty brown or gold. Labrador tea often grows near a look-alike plant, which has a white leaf underbelly instead. Don't use that one! It shouldn't hurt you, but it has no flavour. Early spring is the best time to enjoy a cup of fresh Labrador tea, but you can collect and dry the leaves and have tea for the whole year. Also, don't pick every leaf. These are sensitive plants and it's important to take only what you need.

1 handful fresh Labrador tea leaves

Honey or maple syrup (optional)

The recipe for Labrador tea is easy: break a handful of leaves into your teapot and pour boiling water on top of them. **NOTE:** *Never ever boil the leaves.*

Steep for 10 minutes. Sweeten with maple syrup or honey. Lemon is great in here too.

HAVE FUN! You can play with this recipe, too! I've boiled the flowers with cinnamon sticks, and I've used bird's eye chilies instead of jalapeños. Enjoy!

Fireweed and Jalapeño Jelly

MAKES ENOUGH TO FILL 4 SMALL MASON JARS

Fireweed is so pretty. The young shoots can be cooked and enjoyed in the spring. You can steam them with butter and a little lemon, but they're a real treat pickled, too. Later in the summer, near the middle of July, the flowers come out. I love the light floral flavour the petals lend to baked goods, drinks, and jelly. Fireweed is so named because it loves acidic soils and tends to pop up after a forest fire. The plants will flourish for about five years and then they give way to other brush and bigger trees. The highways of Newfoundland have so much fireweed growing alongside—it's lovely to pass these pinkish-purple stretches of road. This recipe for jelly is a classic; it pops up in tons of Newfoundland plant guides. I've just changed it a little by adding some back heat.

2 ½ cups fireweed juice

1 tsp lemon juice

1 jalapeño, deseeded and finely diced

½ tsp butter

1 ¾ oz dry pectin

3 cups sugar

to make the fireweed juice
Harvest about 8 packed cups of fireweed flowers. Pick all the petals off the stems, as we just want to use the purple petals. Pick out debris, bugs, and brown leaves. Swish these petals around in a bowl of cold water to clean them.

Next, place the cleaned petals in a pot. Fill the pot with water to just below the petals, about 4 cups of water. Boil until the colour seeps from the fireweed flowers and the water is a beautiful lilac colour. **NOTE:** *The petals should look grey and tired.*

Strain the petals out and keep the water. This is your fireweed juice. Now we're ready to make fireweed jelly!

to make the jelly
Begin by warming the fireweed juice, lemon juice, chopped jalapeño, and butter in a pot on the stove. Add dry pectin, bring to boil, and boil hard for 1 minute. Add sugar and bring to full boil again for 1 minute. Skim top of jelly and get all the gunk out of there. Pour into a pitcher and skim again. Fill sterilized jars, leaving a little space at the top. Process in hot water bath for 10 minutes. Let these sit for about 2 days before cracking one open.

Fireweed, Lime, and Mint Simple Syrup

MAKES ENOUGH TO FILL 1 LARGE MASON JAR

By now you've probably figured out that I love floral flavours. I like making this simple syrup and stirring it into a gin-based cocktail.

1 ½ cups fireweed flowers, packed tightly, cleaned, and stems removed

1 cup water, filtered

1 cup granulated sugar

2 tbsp fresh mint or basil

1 tbsp lime juice

You need to spend some time sorting through your flowers. Remove any brown petals, and take the petals off the stems. To clean the petals, place them in a medium-sized bowl and cover with cold water. Leave the flowers to sit in the water for a few minutes, then drain them and set aside.

Add the water and sugar to a medium-sized pot and bring to a boil on the stovetop. Once it's boiling, add the flowers, mint or basil, and lime juice. Boil for 10 to 15 minutes, until all the colour has drained from the flowers. Strain the syrup into a bowl using a fine mesh strainer. Transfer the strained syrup to a sealable container and place in the fridge. Your syrup will last for a few months and is lovely when swirled into a lemonade or cocktail. The syrup can also be frozen and enjoyed as a popsicle!

Fireweed Cocktail

MAKES ENOUGH FOR 1 COCKTAIL

1 ½ oz gin

¾ oz fireweed, lime, and mint simple syrup (see recipe on this page)

1 tsp lime juice

Prosecco, enough to top the glass

Fireweed flowers, dried, for garnish (optional)

Ice

Place all ingredients except Prosecco in a cocktail shaker with plenty of ice and shake well. Fine-strain into a chilled glass. Add a little ice. Top your glass with the Prosecco. This packs a punch!

Rose Petal Iced Tea

MAKES ENOUGH TEA FOR 1 PITCHER

This one is a great summer treat! Pick from wild rose bushes that don't grow near a highway, and make sure that they haven't been sprayed with pesticides. I choose the newly opened petals, not old withering brown ones. Just gently pull the petals from the flower head. You'll want to sort through for bugs and then the rinse the petals under cool water. Use right away for fresh tea!

4 tbsp fresh rose petals

½ tsp pure vanilla extract

2 cups water

1 tbsp honey

1 tbsp lemon juice

Place your rose petals in a teapot. Add vanilla to water and bring to a boil. Pour the boiling water over the rose petals.

NOTE: *Do not boil the rose petals.*

Stir in the honey and lemon juice, cover, and let steep in the fridge for 30 minutes. Strain and serve with ice for a fresh summery tea.

Dried Rose and Red Clover Petal Tea

MAKES ENOUGH FOR 12 CUPS OF STRONG HERBAL TEA

I usually dry rose petals and red clover petals in large batches. Then I mix them with dried mint, chamomile, or pineapple weed, and some catnip for a relaxing tea. Red clover is one of the most easily recognizable foraged goodies, which makes it a great starting place for new foragers. I mostly make tea out of red clover, but sometimes I'll throw the flower heads into a salad, just to brighten things up.

½ cup wild rose petals

½ cup red clover flower heads

¼ cup dried mint, chamomile, or pineapple weed

¼ cup dried catnip

NOTE: *Before I dehydrate flower petals for tea, I always check to make sure that there are no bugs, and I rinse my ingredients in cold water.*

Rinse petals and clover flower heads; let them dry naturally or dab with paper towel.

Then dehydrate in the oven as follows. Line a baking sheet with parchment paper. Preheat the oven to 200°F and lay the petals flat on the parchment paper. **NOTE:** *Don't overcrowd or have overlapping petals. Spread them all out.* Place baking sheet in oven, and check every 10 minutes to see if they are crisp to the touch. This will take 30 minutes at most, but probably far less. Every oven is different, so keep an eye on things!

Now take them out and mix with other dried herbal tea ingredients. I like to crush everything a little with my mortar and pestle. Place your dried rose petals and red clover heads in a teabag. To make tea, you just boil water and pour over the bagged leaves and petals. Sweeten as desired.

FARMING

Large-scale farming for export is not a common practice in Newfoundland. I mean, this is The Rock—land of weathered fishers, kitchen parties, and hundreds of kilometres of exposed, boggy barrens. The wind is harsh and the growing season is frighteningly short. Newfoundland's chief exports have always been fishing, storytelling, and more recently—and controversially—oil. Even small farms have taken a hit in the past few years. From 2011 to 2016, the number of small farms on the island dropped from 510 to 407. More worryingly, about 90 per cent of the fresh vegetables here are imported, arriving by ferry. In worst-case scenarios, where ships are delayed and connection to the mainland is cut off, Newfoundlanders are left with a food supply that will only last a few days.

Luckily, there is new hope for food security! In 2020, there was a massive increase in homesteading and urban gardening. This type of farming is not entirely new to Newfoundland. Fishing families in the early twentieth century used to raise root crops and traded their harvests locally with others. While large-scale farming for export may not be in the immediate future of Newfoundland, a return to home-steading, small farms, and an interest in the "sharing economy" seem to be on the rise. Steve and Lisa McBride added over one thousand new members to their Facebook group, Backyard Farming and Homesteading NL, in a single month. That's about three times the annual growth rate of the group. "The rise in popularity of the group has been surprising," says Steve. "When we moved out to our homestead, I initially expected to be the weird hippie living out in the woods, but there's an entire community—numbering in the thousands—who think the same way I do about producing food locally."

Like many homesteaders, Steve and Lisa do a little bit of everything. They tap their own trees for sap, grow their own mushrooms, keep bees, milk goats, and plant vegetables. They store their harvests in a root cellar. They spend the spring months planting, and the fall is spent pickling and canning. The goal was never to start a business, but to provide for themselves what they need, trading or giving the rest through their social circles. "I really hope that the 'gift economy' catches on" says Steve. "I don't hunt or fish, but I often have an entire freezer of meat gifted to me by fellow homesteaders. We gift our surplus, others give of theirs, and we have a lot of bases covered right off the bat."

I really love the idea of the "sharing" or "gift" economy. After all, sharing, adapting, and problem solving are hallmarks of the culture here. The first harvestable crop in Newfoundland is rhubarb; it grows like a weed here. It's also the vegetable that's gifted to me most often. So here are a few traditional rhubarb recipes, as well as a few with a twist.

The recipe below, or some variation thereof, popped up in over twenty of the cookbooks I examined, and none of them mentioned how much rhubarb chutney the recipe actually made. This recipe may seem wacky, but it works! And it's tasty, but I found the amount of sugar to be a bit intense, and boiling something slowly for an hour seems like a hilarious instruction. In the 2.0 version I've reduced that, and added a few things. Enjoy!

```
              Old-School Rhubarb Chutney
      (Makes enough to fill 2 1/2 medium Mason jars )

  1 1/2 lbs rhubarb, chopped      1 tsp ground ginger
  1 1/2 lbs onions, chopped       1 tsp cloves
  1 lb sugar (brown or white)     1 tsp cinnamon
  1 pint vinegar                  1 tsp salt

          Boil slowly for an hour.
```

Rhubarb Chutney 2.0

MAKES ENOUGH TO FILL 3 MEDIUM MASON JARS

This freezes beautifully, so I usually consume a jar of chutney and freeze the rest.

4 cups washed and coarsely chopped fresh rhubarb

¾ cup sugar

¾ cup cider vinegar

4 cloves garlic, minced

2 tbsp grated fresh ginger

½ tsp ground cumin

½ tsp ground cinnamon

¼ tsp crushed red pepper flakes

1 tsp paprika

¼ tsp ground cardamom

¼ tsp ground cloves

½ cup chopped red onion

⅓ cup sticky raisins

NOTE: *Start by choosing the right rhubarb stalks. Pick the most beautiful bright red stalks for this recipe, otherwise the colour turns a murky brown. Pat them dry after washing them.*

In a large saucepan, combine the sugar, vinegar, garlic, ginger, ground cumin, ground cinnamon, red pepper flakes, paprika, cardamom, and cloves. Bring to a boil. Reduce heat and simmer, uncovered, until sugar is dissolved, about 2 minutes. Add the rhubarb, red onion, and raisins. Cook and stir over medium heat until rhubarb is tender and mixture is slightly thickened, about 20 minutes. Cool completely. Store in the refrigerator, where the chutney will last for several weeks.

Rhubarb Pickles

MAKES ENOUGH TO FILL 3 SMALLISH MASON JARS

I wasn't looking for rhubarb pickle recipes in the archives. I had assumed that it was a recent idea, but I was wrong. Rhubarb pickles popped up over and over again! This is my modern version. It uses less sugar and more spices, and I'd encourage you to try making it with champagne vinegar. It is the perfect rhubarb bite.

2 cups cider vinegar (or champagne vinegar if you're feeling fancy)

1 cup sugar

1 ½ tbsp coarse salt

1 tsp yellow mustard seeds

1 tsp fennel seeds, toasted

2 cloves garlic, sliced

8 whole cloves

10 whole black peppercorns

1 ½-inch piece fresh ginger, peeled and thinly sliced

1 tsp lime juice

1 lb fresh rhubarb, cut into 1-inch pieces (you can substitute ½ lb sliced knotweed if you like)

In a medium saucepan, combine the vinegar, sugar, salt, mustard seeds, toasted fennel seeds, sliced garlic, cloves, peppercorns, ginger, and lime juice. Cook over medium heat, stirring frequently, until the sugar is just dissolved, about 10 minutes. Divide the rhubarb among 3 small, clean glass jars, and pour in the cooled brine mixture. Top with the lids and refrigerate the pickles for 2 days before eating. These will keep for about a month. I use them in salads and on cheese boards.

Rhubarb Strawberry Pie with Maple Whipped Cream

MAKES 1 PIE

There are some great rhubarb pie recipes out there, but of the ones I found, one recipe contained horrifying amounts of sugar, and another involved soaking the rhubarb in vinegar. Mine mixes rhubarb with strawberry, and I also take off the top crust and replace it with maple whipped cream, with some cinnamon and lemon juice to brighten things up.

Pie dough is not the easiest thing to prepare. I've politely swallowed a lot of overworked pie doughs. If you follow this recipe to a T, then you should get pitch-perfect pie dough.

for the crust

2 ½ cups flour

1 tsp salt

1 tbsp sugar

1 cup butter, very cold

4 to 8 tbsp ice water

to make the crust

First, add 1 ½ cups of flour, 1 teaspoon of salt, and 1 tablespoon of sugar to a medium bowl. Whisk for 1 minute so everything is combined. Now grate your very cold butter into the flour mixture, and stir using a wooden spoon. Sprinkle ice water over the mixture. Keep mixing, but don't overdo it.

Remove dough from the bowl and place on a clean surface. Work the dough into a ball. Cut in half and form into two perfectly round disks. Wrap each disk with plastic wrap or beeswax sheets and refrigerate for 3 hours; you can also freeze this dough for later use!

NOTE: *Make your filling while you're waiting for the dough to be perfectly chilled.*

When the dough is ready, roll out a single disk (save the other one for quiche, or a second pie). We want that dough to be fairly thin. Place in pie pan, trim, and use a fork to make an attractive edger.

TIP > Once your crust is on the pie pan, stick it in the freezer for an hour before filling. This should prevent shrinking.

for the filling

2 ½ cups chopped, washed rhubarb (use the reddest parts for best colour)

2 ½ cups washed strawberries, cut into pieces

1 ½ cups brown sugar

2 tbsp cornstarch

1 tbsp flour

½ tsp lime zest

1 tsp lime juice

1 tsp ground cinnamon

1 tsp vanilla extract

3 tbsp butter, cut in small cubes

for the whipped cream

½ cup whipping cream (cold)

1 tbsp maple syrup

1 tsp vanilla

¼ cup icing sugar

Preheat oven to 425°F.

to make the filling

Mix the rhubarb, strawberries, brown sugar, cornstarch, flour, lime zest, lime juice, cinnamon, and vanilla extract thoroughly in a large bowl.

NOTE: *Let this mixture rest for an hour or two, then drain the excess liquid.*

Once your dough has chilled properly, you can pour the filling into the pastry-lined pie plate. Dot the filling with the butter. Cover the whole thing with tinfoil. Place in the oven at 425°F for 15 minutes, then lower the heat to 375°F and bake for 45 minutes. Remove from oven and let cool. Once the filling is chilled, top with maple whipped cream.

to make the whipped cream

Using your stand mixer and the whisk attachment, beat the whipping cream until soft peaks form. Add maple syrup and vanilla. Add the icing sugar in small amounts and beat until peaks hold their shape. Stiff peaks are ideal! Set aside until pie is cooked and chilled, and then top with giant heaps of this whipped cream!

RADISH SALAD

Kat Danylewich submitted the recipe on page 117. I met Kat at a job and fell in love with the way she talked about food. After checking out her social media, I knew I had to ask her to contribute. Her recipes just seemed so fresh and alive. As of this writing, she is about to launch the night menu at Toslow, and I have a feeling that it's going to be inspired.

Here's her story and recipe in her own words:

The first time I had cooked this meal, I was in Montreal for my thirtieth birthday. I was chasing a man I had crossed paths with briefly as I moved to Newfoundland, and he was on his way off the island. It was late August, and it was hot, scorching hot compared to the coastal breezes, and this concrete jungle had us cooked. We were Airbnb hopping for the week, so we could both experience this large city. The travels had me starved, and I couldn't wait to eat. I couldn't wait to cook.

I had been building up all this pressure to be cute and smart and funny, but most of all, I couldn't help thinking to myself, "don't you dare screw up dinner." On this day, we travelled to the Jean-Talon Market and walked around in circles for an embarrassing amount of time. I was a cook, after all. It was full of colour, fresh produce, meats, culture, and intense citrus smells carried throughout as piles of fresh fruit lay cut, waiting to be consumed. I felt overwhelmed, and at least an hour had gone by, maybe two, with nothing inspiring me. I was also consumed by the idea of lugging groceries as we travelled throughout this foreign place.

I wanted something easy, with the least amount of prep and least amount of clean-up, for I wished to make time for slow dancing. It was by the third or fourth walk around that market that my heart had finally stopped and felt settled a feeling of obviousness. There was no question. In front of me lay a large bunch of radishes, white, purple, and red, with the greens still attached. Quickly did all the supporting ingredients fall into place as my friend simply requested shrimp and baguettes. This is where the story ends, though. Imagine such care made to the radish and my guest. Though there is not much left remaining of our friendship, I do love to tell this story. It's not really a story about a woman and a man, but more about a woman and a radish. The humble radish will always wait with patience on store shelves, be consumed raw or braised, dipped in hummus, or shaved bare on top of salad. The radish will always be there for her in every which way she pleases. People will come and go, but radishes are forever.

Warm Radish Salad with Shrimp

Makes enough for 2 to 4 people, as a main

16 to 20 frozen or fresh shrimp, peeled

10 to 12 radishes, greens attached

½ crusty baguette

¼ cup fresh parsley

¼ cup fresh dill

2 cloves garlic, smashed

1 lemon

¾ cup butter

Salt and pepper

Defrost shrimp and remove tails if desired; season with a pinch of salt. Separate the radishes from their greens and wash and dry both. Cut radishes in half and cut the greens into larger bite-sized pieces and set aside. Cube bread into 1-inch pieces and set aside. Chiffonade the parsley and dill, and combine. Smash the cloves of garlic and cut lemon in half.

On low heat, melt butter. Once butter has melted, add shrimp, and stir gently and frequently to ensure they are evenly cooked. Remove from pot with slotted spoon once they are pink and cooked, about 5 to 7 minutes. Turn the heat to medium and add the radishes cut side down. The butter should be slightly bubbling and radishes should be getting some colour. Cook the radishes for about 3 to 4 minutes, until tender but still firm. A knife should easily slide into them. Remove from butter. Place cubed bread in butter and stir gently to coat and soak in the liquids. Season bread with salt and pepper and stir occasionally to ensure all sides are getting toasted. Turn the heat off once the bread has soaked up all of the liquid and bread is nice and toasty.

Add radishes, shrimp, and herbs back to the pot with bread; stir gently to combine. Add the greens, a large pinch of salt and pepper, and the juice from half the lemon. If the pot is not large enough, transfer all ingredients to a large serving bowl. Using your hands or tongs, gently fold the ingredients together and massage the greens.

Serve while still warm.

GARLIC SCAPES AND GARLIC

There's a lot of weird darkness associated with garlic. Greek midwives hung braided garlic bulbs throughout the birthing room to ward off evil spirits. Ancient Greeks used to leave garlic at the crossroads as a meal for the goddess Hecate. In Egypt, King Tutankhamun's tombs were decorated with a scattering of bulbs, and in Central Europe, garlic was thought to ward off the undead. In the writings of Muhammad, it is claimed that garlic came from Satan. When Lucifer was cast out of the garden of Eden and his left foot first touched the earth, garlic pushed through the topsoil.

One must be very suspicious of anyone who does not eat garlic. ROMAN PROVERB

It seems that garlic has been used to fight everything from the common cold to leprosy—Pliny the Elder listed garlic as a cure for 61 different diseases! More recently, garlic has shown itself to be chock-full of antioxidants, seems to improve cholesterol levels, and boosts the immune system.

Garlic is harvested twice. The scapes—long curly green tubular bits at the top of the plant—are harvested in the early summer, and the bulbs themselves get dug up in mid-autumn. Harvesting your scapes is critical; I somehow forgot one year and was left with tiny little bulbs. The plant had expended all of its energy on growing the stems and flowers.

Eat leeks in March and garlic in May,
Then the rest of the year, your doctor can
play. WELSH PROVERB

This is my favourite pickled scape recipe. I don't snack on these scapes whole. I slice them and mix them into potato salad for a bit of garlic bite. I also throw them into grilled cheese sandwiches or salads, and I love them on a cheeseboard.

Quick Pickled Habañero Scapes

MAKES ENOUGH TO FILL 1 LARGE MASON JAR

20 garlic scapes (about one bunch, if you're purchasing from a local market)

½ habañero pepper, sliced into thin rounds

¾ cup cider vinegar

4 tsp fine sea salt

2 tsp sugar

¾ cup water

½ tsp dill seeds, toasted

NOTE: *There may be some extra pickling liquid left over. Just label and store it. You'll find some way to use it up!*

Assemble your ingredients, then rinse your garlic scapes in cold water, dry them, and trim the ends. Stack them into the jar.

TIP > I often leave my scapes whole, but slicing them into bite-sized pieces can make tossing them into salads easier.

Slice the habañero into very skinny rounds. It's a very hot, spicy pepper, so adjust your ratios according to your heat preference! Pack the pepper slices into the jar with the scapes. In a small saucepan over medium-high heat, bring the vinegar, sea salt, sugar, and ¾ cup of water to a simmer. Make sure all the salt and sugar are dissolved. Pour this warm liquid over the scapes and pepper slices. Leave about half an inch at the top and screw the lid closed on the jar. You've just made fridge pickles! They'll be ready to eat in about two weeks and will keep for about a month. You can dig in sooner, but the flavours won't be as beautiful.

POMMES DE TERRE AU GRATIN

This recipe popped up in different versions of the Presbyterian's Ladies Aid cookbook. I had to give it a try. This version is from a 1924 edition. Notice that there are no measurements, no temperatures. I love that laissez-faire approach, but I adapted and played, and my changes are in the 2.0 version.

Old-School Pommes de terre au gratin
(Makes enough for 6 to 8 people, as a side dish)

Butter a baking dish. Place a layer of cold boiled potatoes (sliced), then sprinkle with grated cheese, pepper, salt, and a little flour. Add more layers until dish is filled. Fill with 3/4 cup milk. Dot with butter. Bake in oven for 1/2 hour.

Pommes de Terre au Gratin 2.0
MAKES ENOUGH FOR 6 TO 8 PEOPLE, AS A SIDE DISH

Cooking spray

1 cup diced cooked bacon (about 16 strips)

3 tbsp butter

1 white or yellow onion, diced

7 cloves garlic, minced

¼ cup flour

1 cup chicken stock

2 cups whole milk

1 ½ tsp salt

½ tsp pepper

2 tsp fresh thyme leaves, divided

¼ cup nettle pesto (see page 185 for recipe)

4 lbs Yukon Gold Potatoes, sliced into ⅛-inch rounds

1 ball mozzarella (about ¾ lb), torn into pieces

1 cup grated aged cheddar cheese

½ cup Parmesan cheese, grated

Preheat oven to 400°F. Grease a 13×9-inch baking dish with cooking spray, and set it aside. Now, cook off the bacon. I like to bake my bacon in the oven, as it's already at the perfect temperature. Lay the bacon strips in a single layer, so they don't overlap. Bake until the bacon is crispy, about 10 to 15 minutes, depending on its thickness. Drain the oil off and let bacon cool on paper towel. Chop into ½-inch strips when cool. Reserve.

Melt 3 tablespoons butter in a large sauté pan over medium-high heat. Add onion, and sauté for 7 minutes until soft, caramelized, and translucent. Add garlic and sauté for an additional 1 to 2 minutes until fragrant. Stir in the flour until it is evenly combined, and cook for 1 minute.

Let it simmer, and gradually pour in the stock and whisk until combined. Add in the milk, salt, pepper, and 1 teaspoon of thyme, and whisk until combined. Continue cooking for an additional 1 to 2 minutes until the sauce just barely begins to simmer around the edges of the pan and thickens. Avoid letting it reach a boil. Remove from heat, stir in pesto, and set aside. Spread half of the sliced potatoes in an even layer on the bottom of the pan. Top evenly with half the cream sauce. Add half the bacon. Then sprinkle evenly with half a cup of the mozzarella and half a cup of the cheddar. Add all the Parmesan.

Top evenly with the remaining sliced potatoes, the other half of the cream sauce, the remaining bacon, and the remaining half-cup of both cheeses. Cover the pan with aluminum foil and bake for 30 minutes. The sauce should be nice and bubbly around the edges. Remove the foil and bake uncovered for an additional 25 to 30 minutes, or until the potatoes are cooked through. Transfer the pan to a cooling rack, and sprinkle with the remaining thyme.

OLD-SCHOOL BEET SALAD

I found this in a souvenir cookbook of Fogo Island. So many old "salad" recipes in Newfoundland cookbooks are jellied and horrifying. If you make this recipe, please send me a picture. I gave it a shot, but somehow couldn't get it to set. No serving sizes were given in this monster recipe, so I'm giving my best guess. Also "veggie water"? Is that broth? Or the water that the vegetables in this salad are boiled in? Your guess is as good as mine. The recipe doesn't specify if the vegetables are chopped, but I chopped them into small pieces for my (failed) attempt. I also boiled them first, and treated the water they were boiled in as "veggie water." Good luck and godspeed with this wacky recipe!

Old-School Beet Salad
(Makes enough for 4 to 6 people, as a side dish)

4 tbsp gelatine	2 cups veggie water
1 cup mild vinegar	1/4 cups lemon juice
1 cup sugar	2 tsp salt
1 cup cold water	2 cups carrots
2 cups hot water	6 cups beets

Soften gelatine in cold water for five minutes. Add to soften gelatine stirring well with 2 cups of hot water, 2 cups veggie water, vinegar, lemon juice, sugar, and salt. Cool mixture. When it begins to stiffen add beet and carrot. (If canned vegetables are being used, heat juice to dissolve gelatine.)

New-School Beet Salad

MAKES ENOUGH FOR 2 TO 4 PEOPLE

2 lbs mixed small or medium beets, whole, mixed colours

2 tbsp olive oil, divided, plus more for drizzling

Salt, to taste

¼ cup water

1 batch Lime Chili Dressing (see page 124 for recipe)

4 shishito peppers, sliced into thin rounds

4 radishes

2 tbsp pumpkin seeds

1 orange

½ cup apple chips

Fresh mint leaves (optional)

Preheat oven to 400°F.

NOTE: *Separate your beets by colour; if you roast all the different-coloured beets together on one pan, the colours will bleed together.*

Using separate bowls for each colour of beets, toss your washed beets with 2 tablespoons of olive oil, then lay them in a 13×9-inch baking dish. Season generously with salt. Add the water to the bottom of the baking dish. Cover with tinfoil and roast the beets for 1 hour. Check for doneness with a sharp knife. While the beets are still warm, rub the skins vigorously with paper towel to remove them. Slice into attractive, even pieces. Toss your beets in about half the dressing.

Toss your shishitos in a little bit of olive oil and place on one of the baking sheets you used for your beets. Next, quarter your radishes. Toss with oil and place quartered radishes and shishitos on one half of the baking sheet. Season generously. Pumpkin seeds can go on the other side of the sheet. Roast in 400°F oven for 6 to 8 minutes. Let cool, then chop peppers. Section your orange and grab a small handful of apple chips.

Mix all salad ingredients together and dress with Lime Chili Dressing. Garnish with mint, if you like. I love putting a little goat cheese or Parmesan on this salad, but it's awesome as a vegan dish, too.

Lime Chili Dressing

MAKES APPROXIMATELY 1/2 CUP DRESSING

2 tbsp apple cider vinegar

2 tbsp lime juice

2 tbsp hot chili oil

1 tbsp fresh mint or cilantro, chopped

2 tbsp maple syrup

Whisk together all ingredients.

Beet Soup 2.0 | page 125

Beet Soup 2.0

MAKES ENOUGH FOR 6 PEOPLE

There are a surprising number of beet soup recipes in older Newfoundland cookbooks. Most of them have the same ingredients: beets, onions, beef stock, salt, pepper, and cream. That's fine, but a little expected. My version has fresh dill and sautéed onions, and I like to top it with a homemade garlic sauce—the recipe is below. Also, this soup and the potato buns from the Winter chapter are perfect together.

2 onions, diced

2 tsp salt

2 tbsp canola oil

8 cloves garlic, grated

1 carrot, grated

4 cups grated beets

3 cups vegetable broth

¼ cup apple cider vinegar

Sauté your onions in a tablespoon of oil over medium heat. Add salt while sautéeing onions. Add the grated cloves of garlic to the pot for 1 minute, then add another tablespoon of oil and add your grated carrot. Cook for a few minutes over a medium-high heat, then add grated beets. Toss in the broth and apple cider vinegar. Cook for 30 minutes at a simmer. **NOTE:** *The beets should be just barely cooked, and the broth should be gorgeous and purple.*

I top this with a garlic sauce.

Garlic Sauce   MAKES 4 CUPS

1 cup cloves garlic, peeled

2 ½ tsp salt

3 cups canola oil

½ cup lemon juice

Put peeled garlic cloves in the food processor. Add salt. Process for 2 to 3 minutes until the garlic is finely minced. Slowly, add in one or two tablespoons of oil, then stop and scrape the sides of the bowl using a rubber spatula.

NOTE: *This sauce can separate easily, so go slowly and don't pour all that oil in at once. If the sauce does separate, you can bring it back by slowly adding in a tablespoon of water, but if you're taking your time, you shouldn't have to do that.*

Continue slowly adding oil until things start to look creamy and smooth. Once you're feeling confident that things are emulsifying, add in more oil and process, alternating with the lemon juice. This should take about 20 minutes. Go slow! I love this sauce with beets, but it's also beautiful with lamb, chicken, you name it. Sometimes I just dip crackers into it.

TURNIP TREAT

I was absolutely delighted to discover that there's a town in Newfoundland called Turnip Cove. Turnips are easy to grow here. They love the rocky hard soil. I used to hate turnip, but that's only because I've only had it boiled to death and mushed with salt beef Jigg's Dinner liquid. Here's a turnip treat recipe from the 1940s that I enjoy, and then a modern twist on it. This makes enough for 4 people, as a side dish.

1 medium turnip

1/2 tsp sugar

1 tbsp butter

Salt and pepper

Pare off half inch of turnip peel. Cut in pieces about size of potato chips. Cook in small amount of boiling water with sugar. Drain and mash with butter, salt, and pepper.

Modern Turnip Treat with Miso and Lime

MAKES ENOUGH FOR 2 TO 3 PEOPLE, AS A SIDE DISH

1 lb small white turnips, trimmed, scrubbed, and quartered

2 tbsp white miso

2 tbsp butter

1 tbsp maple syrup

Salt and pepper, to taste

2 tbsp fresh lime juice

NOTE: *First, you should know that this can work with traditional turnips, but it's so much more fun with the beautiful little white turnips. If you're using regular turnips, please cut them into wedges or cubes. Small white baby turnips can be quartered.*

Combine the baby turnips or wedges with miso, butter, and maple syrup in a medium pan. Add just enough water to cover the turnips. Season with salt and pepper. Go a bit heavy with the pepper. Bring to a boil over medium-high heat and cook the turnips, turning occasionally, until they are tender and the liquid has evaporated, about 15 to 20 minutes. Once all the liquid has cooked off, keep cooking the turnips until they are caramelized and the sauce thickens and glazes the vegetables, about 5 minutes longer. Add lime juice. Season with salt and pepper again. Serve.

I really like this alongside pan-fried cod.

OLD-SCHOOL PARSNIP BALLS

I found this 1941 recipe in my final round of edits for this cookbook, but I couldn't not include it! Usually parsnips are overlooked or ignored entirely, but this ingenious recipe makes them the star!

1 lb parsnips
1 tsp salt
2 tbsp butter
2 tbsp milk
1/2 tsp pepper
1 egg
Breadcrumbs

Mash parsnips with salt, pepper, butter, and milk. Form into balls. Dip in beaten egg and roll in bread crumbs. Drop into deep fat and fry until golden brown.

This old-school recipe got me thinking about how to turn all the attention to parsnip. I added apple for acidity and sweet vanilla to balance the soup below.

Candied Parsnip 2.0 Apple and Vanilla Soup

MAKES ENOUGH FOR 4 TO 6 PEOPLE

6 medium parsnips, chopped

1 tbsp olive oil

1 tbsp brown sugar

Pinch ground cloves

3 tbsp butter

1 onion, diced

2 celery stalks, chopped

2 apples, Gala or Honeycrisp

3 cups chicken broth

1 vanilla bean, scraped

Salt and pepper, to taste

Apple chips for garnish (optional)

Preheat oven to 400°F and line a baking sheet with parchment paper. Toss the parsnips with olive oil and brown sugar. Sprinkle just the tiniest bit of cloves onto the parsnips. Roast in the oven for about 30 minutes until they caramelize. We want a healthy browning on them. In a large pot over medium heat, melt your butter and heat the pan well. Add onion and sauté until completely translucent. Now add celery and apples, and let these cook for about 5 minutes. Add broth and parsnips and bring to a boil. Reduce the heat to low and let simmer for about 30 minutes. Scrape the vanilla bean into the pot. Season with salt and pepper to taste, then take the whole thing off the stove and let it cool. Working in batches, purée until it's completely smooth.

I like to garnish this with small apple chips.

FISHING

Most fisheries open in the spring and last throughout the summer. There is the cod fishery, the capelin industry, squid jigging, and handlining. There are mussels you can harvest by hand in Twillingate and cultivated oysters from Merasheen Bay. Traditionally in Newfoundland, however, when we talk about "fish," we're talking about cod, and when we talk about cod, we're talking about politics. Since this is a cookbook, the focus here will be on how to get and prepare cod for a meal.

I will say that while I'm a huge fan of cod, I am worried about the industry as a whole. Gill nets, in particular, get a thumbs-down from me. Gill nets are long curtains of netting that get suspended vertically in the water by buoys. The nets are pretty much impossible to see, so fish swim right into them. It's a patently unfair human advantage. In theory, these nets are just for catching cod, but other animals can get twisted and entangled. Additionally, the idea that a fresh cod might spend a day or two struggling to death in these nets stresses me out. It's not an exceptionally humane death, and the adrenalin that surges in the cod while it tries to escape the net affects the flavour.

I prefer handlined cod. It's more humane, and the meat is fresh and delicious. I went handlining with QV Charters, and they fried up some fresh, beer-battered, handlined cod for me, and it was the best I've ever had, so I've included their beer-battered cod recipe.

Deep-Fried Cod Recipe from the Folk at QV Charters

MAKES ENOUGH FOR 2 TO 4 PEOPLE

A couple of hints regarding this recipe. I like to let the batter sit for a few minutes before dipping my fish. I think this helps the batter breathe and makes for a puffier bite. Also, try to use local cod. Cod that's been shipped from Norway is still tasty, but supporting local fishers is best. Finally, make sure you dry your cod well before dipping, and don't over-crowd the pan.

¾ cup all-purpose flour

Salt and pepper, to taste

½ tsp seafood seasoning blend

1 tsp garlic powder (optional)

¾ cup beer (I don't love using an IPA or Sour, but everything else works)

1 large egg, beaten

1 lb cod, cut into 6 pieces

Vegetable oil, for frying

Lemon wedges, for serving

In a large bowl, whisk together the dry ingredients, then whisk in the beer and egg. Let the batter rest for about 15 minutes. Dry the cod really well; pat it with paper towels. Heat about 3 or 4 inches of vegetable oil in a deep pan to 375°F. Be extra careful—oil burns are a special kind of pain! Coat your cod pieces in the tasty batter and drop them into the oil. **NOTE: *Do this in batches! Don't crowd the pan.*** Fry until golden and fish is cooked through. Remove and place on a paper-towel-lined cutting board. Let it rest for a minute and then season. Serve with fries, a good beer, and lemon wedges.

The codfish lays a thousand eggs,
the homely hen lays one
The codfish never cackles, to tell you when she's done
And so we scorn the codfish,
while the humble hen we prize
Which only goes to show you that it pays to advertise.

TRADITIONAL RHYME

In this section, I also pay attention to my favourite seafood: crab and lobster. These fisheries usually open in April, and I look forward to this all year. In a non-pandemic year, my friends and I would gather, crack open bottles of wine, jam up the tunes, and don our garbage bags. It's the only way to eat crab and lobster, as the juices drip all over. I like to make homemade fries and garlic aïoli, and I wash it all down with something a little sweet, maybe a Riesling, to cut through the buttery richness.

The trouting season opens up in the spring and lasts into the summer. I often spend a few days soaking wet at 4 a.m. as my friends and I try to find one of our secret fishing holes. I didn't include any trout recipes because I cook mine up in the woods, over a flame, or on the cast-iron pan in my house. I keep it pretty simple with trout, adding just lemon, flour, and butter. The pan bread recipe that I mentioned earlier in this chapter? That's the perfect thing to eat alongside some fresh trout.

Capelin is another seasonal treat that comes tumbling into the shallow beaches to spawn. Whales are close behind, as capelin is one of their primary sources of food. These little fish are a cultural moment. Every summer, word gets out that the capelin are rolling, and my friends and I head to Middle Cove with our nets and our fire-making supplies. The beach is lined with hundreds of folks who had the same ideas, and the shore is alight with small fires and the smell of tiny fish being grilled. Although I love harvesting capelin, I didn't participate last year, and I won't join for the foreseeable future, as the capelin industry seems to be in a state of collapse. Capelin stocks are down, and this little fish's future seems grim, with conservation groups calling for a moratorium on the commercial harvest. Although individual harvesting probably has a negligible impact when compared to the industry as a whole, I'll probably aim to stay out of the water for a few years to come.

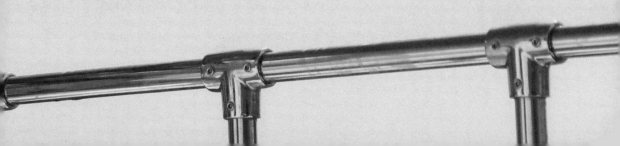

OLD-SCHOOL FRIED COD TONGUES

I found this recipe in a souvenir cookbook from Fogo Island. Sometimes the older recipes are perfect in their simplicity. Also, did you know that cod tongues aren't actually tongues? They are just a delicious muscle in the cod's neck.

Carefully wash fresh cod tongues and dry in paper towel. Allow 7 or 8 per person. Put 1 1/2 cups flour, 1 tsp salt, and 1/2 tsp pepper together in a paper bag. Put tongues in and shake until evenly floured. Cut up 1/2 lb pound salt pork and fry until golden brown. Remove pork cubes and fry tongues until golden brown on both sides. Serve with mashed potatoes and green peas.

Pan-Fried Cod Tongues with Farro, Mint, Capers, and Salt Pork

MAKES ENOUGH FOR 4 PEOPLE

Farro is such an underrated grain! It's full of fibre and the texture goes so well with tongues. This recipe is a little out there, but I think it works. You could also take out the capers and use garlic scapes instead.

2 tbsp pine nuts

2 cups farro

6 cups vegetable broth, or water

2 tbsp lemon zest

2 tbsp lemon juice

3 tbsp olive oil

1 tsp capers

Salt and pepper, to taste

1 tsp diced salt pork fat

8 to 12 cod tongues (3 to 4 per serving)

2 tbsp butter

1 tbsp parsley

1 tbsp fresh mint leaves, roughly chopped

Begin by toasting your pine nuts. I do this on the stovetop, so I can keep an eye on the whole thing. Once they've toasted, set aside.

Add 2 cups farro to a pot with 6 cups of vegetable broth. Bring to a boil and then reduce heat to a simmer. Cook until the grains are tender, about 30 minutes. Drain the water and set aside. Now mix in lemon zest, lemon juice, olive oil, and capers. Season the farro with salt and pepper to taste. Pan-fry the diced pork fat over medium heat until brown and caramelized. Stir this into the farro mixture.

Pat cod tongues as dry as possible. Using a good heavy-duty pan, heat up the butter. Once the frying pan is good and hot, lightly season the cod tongues and lower into the pan. Fry for 3 minutes on each side, turning them with kitchen tongs as necessary, until they are golden, brown, and delicious. Toss the cod tongues into the farro mixture and garnish with parsley, mint, and pine nuts. This is a real treat, so enjoy!

COD AU GRATIN

It shouldn't work. The flavours in this dish have no business working, but somehow, they do. Before I moved here, I thought fish and cheese were strange bedfellows. Now, I'm converted and it's one of my favourite Newfoundland dishes. I found dozens of cod au gratin recipes, but the one listed below popped up everywhere. My 2.0 version is baked into a pastry crust and fancied up slightly.

4 tbsp butter

2 tbsp flour

1 tsp salt

1/2 tsp pepper

1 cup cheddar cheese, grated

2 cups milk

2 1/2 cups fresh codfish, cooked, flaked, and cooled

Melt butter, add flour, salt, and pepper, stir to make a paste. Add milk and cook until it thickens, stirring constantly. Grease a 2-quart casserole. Pour a little sauce over the bottom of the pot. Add a layer of codfish, sprinkle with cheese. Repeat these layers until all ingredients are used, ending with a layer of cheese. Bake in a moderate oven (350°F) until brown, about 30 minutes.

Cod au Gratin 2.0 Pie with Homemade Breadcrumbs

MAKES ENOUGH FOR 1 PIE, OR 6 PEOPLE

I've tested a lot of cod au gratin recipes for this book. I've fooled around with ratios and teased out the Dijon and tested all the different kinds of cheese. I know it seems incredibly biased considering we share a publisher, but Barry Parsons's recipe for cod au gratin is my all-time favourite. I've turned Barry's cod au gratin recipe into a pie. I've also changed the cheese, gone with a whole-grain Dijon mustard, and added homemade cracker crumbs. Other than those swaps, though, I follow Barry's cod au gratin recipe. It's never let me down.

1 pie crust (see recipe on page 114)

for the filling

2 cups whole milk

3 tbsp butter

3 tbsp flour

1 tsp grated lemon zest

2 tbsp whole-grain Dijon mustard

1 tsp summer savoury, or use dill or tarragon as substitutes

Salt and pepper, to taste

½ cup grated Parmesan cheese

3 lbs fresh cod fillets

1 ½ cups shredded aged cheddar (I use an applewood-smoked cheddar)

1 cup homemade cracker crumbs (see savoury cracker recipe, page 37)

1 tbsp olive oil

to make the crust

To begin, we're going to make the crust from the rhubarb strawberry pie recipe earlier in this chapter. Follow those instructions exactly to make your crust. Then, we make the filling.

to make the pie

Preheat oven to 350°F. Scald the milk in the microwave for 4 to 5 minutes. In a medium saucepan over a low-medium heat, add the butter and flour and cook together for 2 minutes. Slowly pour in the scalded milk, whisking constantly. Cook until the sauce begins to thicken. Add the lemon zest, whole-grain Dijon mustard, and savoury, and season with salt and pepper to taste. Add the Parmesan cheese to the sauce.

Arrange the fish in the bottom of the cooled pie crust. Pour the sauce over the fish. Top with the shredded cheddar cheese. Mix the cracker crumbs with the olive oil and sprinkle over the cheese. You can add a little extra savoury to the crumbs if you like, about half a teaspoon or so. Bake for 45 to 60 minutes at 350°F, until it's bubbling and the top has evenly browned. Enjoy!

Grilled Lobster Tails with Lemon Lobster Butter

MAKES ENOUGH FOR 4 PEOPLE

There are boiled lobster and crab recipes aplenty in the older books. I'm a huge fan of both, but grilled feels a little fancier! Give this a try!

4 lobster tails, fresh or thawed from frozen

4 lemon wedges

Lemon Lobster Butter (see recipe on page 141)

First, we have to get the tail meat out of the shell, intact! Use a knife to cut along the top of the tail, without cutting all the way through. Remove the vein if you see one. To remove the meat from the tail, loosen the meat with your fingers and pull it out in one whole section. Line the tails up in a shallow tray and add some of the butter to each tail. I use about a tablespoon on each one.

Heat the grill to high, then grill the lobster tails for 10 mins until cooked through. Put them on plates, garnish with lemon wedges, and serve the remaining lemon lobster butter on the side for dipping.

I love pairing lemony lobster with a fancy spicy and sweet white wine like Gewürztraminer, but you can't go wrong with a buttery Chardonnay, either.

Lemon Lobster Butter

MAKES ENOUGH FOR 4 LOBSTER TAILS

½ cup butter, softened

5 cloves garlic, chopped

1 tsp lemon juice

1 tsp lemon zest

1 tsp ground lemon peppercorn or ground alder

½ tsp cayenne pepper

½ tsp seafood seasoning blend

½ tsp salt

A dash paprika (optional)

Add all ingredients to bowl of stand mixer. Using the paddle attachment, mix all ingredients together and set aside. Store mixture in fridge until an hour or so before it's needed, then remove from fridge to soften butter before use.

Autumn

FALL FRUITS AND VEGETABLES

You'll notice that this chapter is much larger than the others. Fall, in my opinion, is the best and brightest season for cooking, and it's my favourite. I spend most of these months out on the hills and barrens, picking and hunting for berries and mushrooms. Hunting season for small and large game opens up, the food fishery is given its final hurrah for a single week in September, and the market stands are bright with the beautiful colour palette of fall vegetables.

Let's chat berries first. In August and September, I spend almost all of my free time picking. The night before a berry-picking adventure, I'll download podcasts and charge my phone. In the morning I don my Tilley hat, slather myself with sunscreen, and pack a slew of snacks and water. Then, I head out to one of my favourite berry patches. I tend to drop a pin on Google maps—a modern version of leaving bread-crumbs—to track my location. I want one of my close friends to be able to find me if I wander too far, get lost in the bramble, or run into fairies.

Usually, I like to pick near the ocean. It's the best when I can see big waves crash onto the rocky shore as I work. I also love bumping into other berry-picking folks filling up their respective salt beef buckets. We give each other a little nod of recognition and a friendly "some day for it." Occasionally, I'll trek inland, foraging for treats amid the bogs and barrens and wandering down ATV tracks, but it's not my preference. There are too many mosquitoes and I'm a little worried about getting lost.

On an ideal berry-picking day, there will be sun overhead and a cool breeze. I'll pick a few litres, maybe a gallon. The goal for berry-picking season? To pick enough for the entire year. I want my freezer overflowing.

Autumn is my favourite time of year to be in the kitchen, and I'll spend most weekends cooking pies, jams, mustards, and scones.

I also want to give berries and homemade treats away as gifts. After all, the berries in my larder cost nothing but time, so I'll want to squander them freely. To justify this sharing, I make sure I have a freezer full. So, here's what I pick and what I make.

SERVICEBERRIES

I tend to pick serviceberries (more commonly known as the chuckley pear or saskatoon berry) in early August. The serviceberry supposedly received its name because its spring flowering would let folks in northern climates know that the ground was soft enough to dig graves for those who had died over the winter. I've seen this claim in a slew of books, but couldn't track down any first-hand sources to verify. Serviceberries look like blueberries, but really seem more like little apples or cherries to me. I pick a little less than a gallon, dehydrate them in an oven overnight, and then treat them like currants. They dot my cinnamon buns, breads, and loaves. I stir them into granola. It is nice to have some of these on hand, but I don't feel devastated if I accidentally miss the season—which sometimes happens.

BLACKBERRIES

A good blackberry patch is the holy grail of foraging. I've stumbled upon a handful on the Avalon Peninsula, but they are few and far between. If you find one, keep it a secret. Blackberries loom large in mythology and religion, especially Christianity. Different churches claim that Christ's crown of thorns was made from blackberry runners. In Greek mythology, blackberries have their own symbolism. In one famous tale, Bellerophon, a Greek hero and demigod, attempts to ride Pegasus to Mount Olympus, but falls and becomes injured upon landing in a blackberry bush. His wounds are a punishment for his arrogance, and blackberries have been linked to hotheads, injuries, and the pride that comes before a fall ever since.

Blackberries have canes, intense prickles, toothed leaves, and gorgeous bumpy juicy black fruit. The berries will be green at first, turn red, and finally black. They ripen at the end of August and stay ripe for about two weeks. They look just like raspberries, save for the colour difference. Also, a quick heads-up: please wear long pants and long sleeves. These brambles want to leave scars; they demand a blood sacrifice. You can do a thousand things with blackberries, but I like pairing them with lime curd, whipped cream, and homemade pavlovas. Also, I know that it isn't especially groundbreaking to pair a berry chutney with moose meat, but blackberries do sing with game meat.

BLUEBERRIES

The town of Oxford, Nova Scotia, has a giant blueberry guarding it. The blueberry is smiling widely and waving furiously; it walks a very fine line between adorably campy and completely hideous. When visitors drive into Oxford, they are also greeted by a sign that proudly proclaims Oxford as the "blueberry capital of the world." It always makes me feel a little angry. After all, that is a very bold claim and I refuse to believe it. Newfoundland blueberries are the most delicious and abundant in the world. Full stop.

Blueberry recipes punctuate old cookbooks because berry picking and preserving the berry harvest was an important part of surviving a winter in Newfoundland. Whole families spent their autumns wandering the barrens, picking their fill, and selling to those who couldn't. Myths and lore are also connected to these recipes. Fairy stories in particular seem to be linked to berry picking, and served as warnings to children against wandering alone in the woods. Children were told not to stray too far or "the fairies might get ya!"

BAKEAPPLES

The bakeapple is the one berry that I don't forage for. Don't get me wrong, I'm a bakeapple fan. I love these little peach-coloured beauties. I just don't know of any secret bakeapple spots. Instead, I usually end up buying them on the side of the road from the back of someone's truck. Bakeapples are known as cloudberries in other parts of the world. They made headlines a few years back when the chefs at the world-famous NOMA in Copenhagen made a bakeapple soup dessert featuring a snowy island of frozen yoghurt and candied pine cones as trees. I haven't done anything as fun with them, but I have paired a chia seed bakeapple jam with cardamom buttermilk waffles and whipped cream. You'll find that jam recipe in this book.

PARTRIDGEBERRIES

I used to loathe the partridgeberry. To me, partridgeberries smell like feet. They do! They smell like someone was in a rush to go outside and jammed their feet into a pair of winter boots without socks. It's pretty loathsome. Also, the flavour of these little red berries is so tart that I was convinced I needed to compensate with sugar and as a result, I made some pretty disgusting jams for a while. However, I've learned to love it! Once you know how to work with it, that tartness livens everything up.

The partridgeberry is found all over the world, but goes by other names. In Nordic countries, the partridgeberry is known as the lingonberry; it's turned into sweet soups and cordials, and served alongside game meats like elk and reindeer. Closer to home, Nova Scotians call it the foxberry, and in different parts of the United States it's called the cowberry or mountain cranberry. It's important to note that partridgeberries do contain worms, so you have to wait until after the first frost to pick these beauties. The worms have left and the berries are ready to eat.

Finally, I'd like to mention a few obvious but important housekeeping notes on berry picking: try not to get lost, don't litter, and be as careful and safe as possible. Getting lost can end very poorly, so drop "pins," pick with your friends, and stay on the trails. Second, all the milk of human kindness that I possess tends to dissipate into the thin pale juice of bitter loathing when I come across stray chip bags in the woods. Take out what you've brought in! Don't leave anything behind. Finally, don't ever pick or eat anything that you're not 100 per cent confident in identifying.

Enjoy berry season, everyone! It's so short and sweet.

Blueberry Leaf Tea

MAKES 1 CUP OF TEA

Blueberry leaves have a very grassy flavour, so I like to mix them with a few other things before making them into tea. I cannot find any historical recipes using the leaves of the plant, so here's my own.

1 tsp finely chopped fresh or dried blueberry leaves per cup of tea

½ tsp dried mint OR 1 tsp fresh mint

½ tsp dehydrated blueberries

½ tsp chamomile flowers

Place all ingredients in tea bag. Boil water. Pour over teabag. Steep in near-boiling water for about 5 minutes before serving. Sweeten with honey or maple syrup if desired.

Spiced Blueberries

MAKES ENOUGH TO FILL 6 MEDIUM MASON JARS

While I didn't find any recipes for actual shrubs (a type of historical liqueur or syrup) on any of my trips to the archives, I did find dozens of recipes for blueberries pickled with apple cider vinegar that very much read like a shrub recipe. This particular recipe works beautifully in cocktails, but these spiced blueberries also pair well with game and are amazing in a salad. The Spiced Blueberry-Basil Shrub recipe on page 152 makes a more reasonable amount and has a slightly more complex flavour.

6 cups sugar

2 cups cider vinegar

10 cups blueberries

2 tbsp cinnamon

1 tsp ground cloves

Dissolve sugar in vinegar, then add other ingredients and boil for 1 hour. Ladle the pickled berries into the Mason jars, leaving about half an inch of space at the top. Place the sterilized lids and screw on the rings. Fill a giant stockpot halfway full with water. Bring water to a boil over high heat and lower your jars into the pot. **NOTE:** *The water level should be about 1 inch over the top of the jars, so you may need to add more water.*

Bring the water to a full boil. Cover your pot with a lid, and boil for 15 minutes. **NOTE:** *You might need to do this in batches, depending on the size of your stockpot.*

Remove jars and allow to cool. Ensure that jars are all sealed properly and airtight.

Spiced Blueberry-Basil Shrub

MAKES ENOUGH TO FILL 2 SMALL MASON JARS

1 ½ cups blueberries
1 cup apple cider vinegar
1 cup sugar
1 tbsp red chili flakes
1 tbsp basil, chopped
1 tbsp maple syrup

Put the blueberries and 1 tablespoon of the vinegar in a food processor. Pulse the berries just enough to break them up. In a medium saucepan, combine the pulsed berries with the remaining vinegar, the sugar, red chili flakes, chopped basil, and maple syrup. Bring to a simmer over medium heat, then reduce to low and cover the pot. Cook for half an hour, stirring occasionally. Transfer the hot sauce to a blender. Blend the shrub to get it as smooth as possible, then pass it through a fine mesh strainer directly back into the pan. Simmer over medium-low heat, stirring occasionally, until it has reduced by about one-third of its original volume. **NOTE:** *This will take about 15 minutes. It should coat the back of a spoon and have the viscosity of syrup.*

Let the shrub rest at least overnight before using. Covered, it will keep for about a month in the refrigerator.

Blueberry Jam-Filled Buns

MAKES 8 BUNS

I found jam-filled bun recipes everywhere; this is a version I liked best.

2 cups flour

4 tsp baking powder

½ tsp salt

2 tbsp sugar

½ cup butter

1 egg

½ cup milk, plus extra to brush the tops

¼ tsp cinnamon

8 tbsp blueberry jam, or 1 tbsp per bun

Preheat oven to 425°F, and grease a baking sheet. Blend flour, baking powder, salt, and half the sugar together. Cut butter into the dry ingredients. Beat the egg and milk together, then make a well in the centre of the dry ingredients and add the egg and milk mixture. Knead for 10 seconds. Roll out onto a floured pastry cloth so that it's about half an inch thick. Cut with a 2-inch round cutter. Brush tops with milk and dip into a mixture of cinnamon and the rest of the sugar. Place each round on the cookie sheet. Make a deep well in the middle of each round with your thumb, then fill it with blueberry jam, about a tablespoon per bun. Bake for about 12 minutes.

Blueberry Jam-Filled Scones

MAKES 8 SCONES

Okay, so the blueberry jam bun recipe that I found was intriguing, but I've mixed it up here and turned those buns into scones. You just slice the scone open on one end, stuff with jam, and voilà! A beautiful tea time treat!

2 cups flour

⅓ cup granulated sugar

1 tbsp baking powder

½ tsp baking soda

½ tsp salt

½ cup cold salted butter

1 large egg

⅔ cup buttermilk

1 vanilla bean, scraped

1 cup blueberries

1 handful toasted almonds or some turbinado sugar

Preheat oven to 400°F and line a baking sheet with parchment paper. Add flour, sugar, baking powder, baking soda, and salt to a medium-sized mixing bowl and stir to combine. I usually whisk the dry ingredients together, just to get some air in there. Grate the very cold butter into the flour mixture using a cheese grater.

In a separate bowl, add egg, buttermilk, and vanilla. Beat the wet ingredients together with a whisk. Make a well in the middle of the flour mixture and pour in the liquid mixture, reserving about two tablespoons to use as an egg wash. Fold with a wooden spoon. It is really important not to overwork the dough. Now, add the blueberries!

NOTE: *It is important not to mix the blueberries into this dough too early, as you don't want all your dough to turn blue.*

Turn the dough out onto a well-floured board, and fold it over itself about 2 to 3 times; this helps to create layers. Shape the dough into a circle about 1 ½ inches thick, then cut into 8 large scones. Place the scones on the prepared baking sheet, brush the top with the reserved egg wash, and sprinkle generously with either turbinado sugar or toasted almonds. Bake for 20 minutes until scones are golden brown and a toothpick inserted in the centre comes out clean. Let cool completely on a wire rack.

Once the scones are cool, cut each one horizontally three-quarters through, and spread with a thick layer of blueberry jam. I like to get decadent and serve these with whipped cream.

Blueberry Jam-Filled Scones | page 155

BLUEBERRY CAKE FROM 1905

This recipe first appeared in a Newfoundland cookbook in 1905—it's one of my all-time favourite recipes. It's bewildering to behold. There's no ingredient list. Why beat each egg separately? Why is a coffee cup of sugar a measurement? How big was a coffee cup in 1905? What the heck is a clear icing?

One coffee cup of sugar, one-third cup of butter, one and half cups of sifted flour, two teaspoons of baking powder, three eggs beaten separately, half teaspoon of lemon flavouring, the cup of blueberries, bake half an hour. While hot, ice with clear icing.

Blueberry Cake 2.0

MAKES ONE 9-INCH CAKE

As you can see, recreating old recipes involves a great deal of guesswork and conjecture. I did my best to recreate the blueberry cake of 1905, but it fell a bit flat. Delicious, but too dense. I decided to update the recipe by treating the original as a spine, adding my own columns as I made changes that I feel reflect our time period. Thyme and almonds were added to the cake, and instead of lemon extract, I added a tablespoon of local maple syrup, although bourbon could also be fun. I played around with the ratios and gave the surface a crunchy topping as opposed to the vague "clear icing" listed in the original recipe. The result is a moist, modern blueberry cake that harkens to way back when. Save the crumbs for your pocket if you're enjoying it in the woods!

for the topping

½ cup unsalted butter

½ cup white granulated sugar

1 cup large flake oats, toasted

2 tsp flour

1 cup sliced almonds

1 tbsp heavy cream

Thyme (to garnish)

to make the topping

We start with browning the butter for the topping. Melt butter in a pot at a medium heat, keeping a close eye on it. You'll want to take it off the heat when the butter releases a nutty smell and is a nice tan colour. Remove from heat and keep the browned butter at room temperature. About 10 minutes before the cake is done, combine all the topping ingredients except for the thyme in the pan with the browned butter. Return to stovetop on medium-high heat until it starts to bubble. Reduce heat to a simmer and cook for 3 minutes, stirring once or twice carefully, trying not to break any of the sliced almonds.

for the filling
3 large eggs

1 cup sugar

1 tsp baking powder

½ tsp salt

½ cup unsalted butter, melted

1 tsp vanilla extract

1 tsp maple syrup

1 ¼ cups flour

1 cup fresh blueberries

to make the cake
Preheat oven to 350°F. Grease a 9-inch springform pan with cooking oil and line the bottom of the pan with parchment paper. Beat the eggs and sugar together until pale yellow, about 5 minutes. Add the baking powder and salt and stir in. In a separate bowl, stir the melted butter, vanilla, and maple syrup (if using) together, then add it to the egg mixture. Beat to incorporate, then add the flour and mix until absorbed.

NOTE: *Do not overmix here! Beating every single lump out of a cake batter will result in too much gluten and a tough cake!*

Pour the batter into the prepared springform pan and spread evenly. Sprinkle the blueberries over the top, then press them into the batter. Bake for 40 to 45 minutes in oven or until the cake is puffy in the middle and just starting to turn golden brown on the edges.

put them together
Once the cake is just barely done, pull it out of the oven and increase the heat to 400°F. Carefully spoon the topping ingredients over the cake. Return cake to the oven and bake for an additional 10 minutes. Let it cool for 15 to 20 minutes before removing from springform pan. Garnish with thyme and serve!

Cream Cheese Blueberry Pie **MAKES ONE 9-INCH PIE**

This recipe is based on a famous pie. The Preserve Company of New Glasgow, Prince Edward Island, has a raspberry cream cheese pie on their menu that is just absolute perfection. I've taken that recipe, changed it a bit, and used Newfoundland blueberries instead. I hope you like it.

1 pie crust (see recipe on page 114)

for the filling
½ cup heavy whipping cream

4 oz cream cheese, softened

½ cup icing sugar

⅔ cup granulated sugar

¼ cup cornstarch

½ cup water

¼ cup lemon juice

3 cups blueberries

to make the crust
To begin, we're going to make the crust from the rhubarb strawberry pie recipe, found on page 114. Follow those instructions exactly to make your crust. Once the dough has chilled, roll it out and transfer to a 9-inch plate. Refrigerate for 2 hours. Preheat oven to 425°F. Put parchment paper over the crust and fill with pie weights. Bake for 25 minutes. Remove from oven and take out the weights. Let cool completely before filling.

to make the filling
Whip your cream until you have stiff peaks that hold their shape. In a small bowl, beat your cream cheese and icing sugar together until smooth. Fold in whipped cream, and ensure mixture is free of lumps. Spread over the pie crust that has been cooked and chilled.

In a large saucepan over medium heat combine the sugar, cornstarch, water, and lemon juice until smooth, then stir in blueberries. Bring to a boil over medium heat, stirring constantly for 3 minutes. Let cool completely. Spread blueberry mixture over top of cream cheese layer. Let the entire pie sit for 3 hours before eating, so everything will set.

BAKEAPPLE JAM

Ah, another recipe written in a confusing paragraph style; that seems to be a trend with these recipes from the 1970s. This is another one from my mother-in-law, but similar versions can be found everywhere.

Wash and weigh berries. Add 3/4 pound of sugar to each pound of berries. Place both together in a container and let stand overnight. Next morning put on to cook, bringing the jam slowly to a boil. Boil slowly for 20 minutes. Pour into hot sterilized jars and seal.

Bakeapple Jam 2.0

MAKES ENOUGH TO FILL 2 SMALL MASON JARS

The recipe above is very sweet. Here's my reduced-sugar version, with chia seeds for added fibre and flavour. This is very much a fridge/freezer jam. My favourite kind! I'll go through the full hot water processing about twice a year, but I prefer jams that I can freeze. This will last three weeks in the fridge.

4 cups bakeapples

½ cup sugar, or more/less to taste

3 tbsp water

1 tbsp chia seeds

Take all ingredients, except for the chia seeds, and add them to the pot. Bring the pot to a simmer over medium heat.

NOTE: *Stir occasionally, as sometimes the bakeapples can cling to the bottom of the pot.*

Cook for about 20 minutes, then add the chia seeds and simmer for 5 more minutes. Pour jam into jars, and place in fridge, where it should set. This will be food safe for about 2 to 4 weeks in the fridge, but it also freezes beautifully!

Partridgeberry Pickles

MAKES ENOUGH TO FILL 6 MEDIUM MASON JARS

Versions of this recipe were found in a slew of older cookbooks. I've combined the essentials into one.

6 cups partridgeberries

6 cups chopped onions

4 cups sugar

½ cup vinegar

1 tsp salt

1 tsp cinnamon

2 tsp pickling spices

Put berries, onions, and sugar to soak in vinegar overnight. Next day, put it all in a pot, add the other ingredients, and boil until berries and onions are soft. Put in sterilized bottles and seal. Older cookbooks will tell you that these pickles will keep for years. I would urge you to ignore these instructions! Follow current best practices for preserving and consuming.

Partridgeberry Pickles 2.0

MAKES ENOUGH TO FILL 1 MEDIUM MASON JAR

I love the bones of this recipe, so I made a few adjustments and additions here and there. I'd consume the preserves within a month, but wait a week first so the flavour can develop.

6 tbsp champagne vinegar or white wine vinegar

2 tbsp fish sauce

2 tbsp sugar

3 tbsp water

Pinch ground cloves

¾ cup partridgeberries

Combine vinegar, fish sauce, sugar, water, and cloves in a jar. Close well and shake vigorously until all sugar is dissolved. Add partridgeberries and press down to submerge in liquid. Seal jar and chill for at least 4 hours. These will keep for about a month. They also freeze well!

Partridgeberry Cheesecake

MAKES ONE 9-INCH CHEESECAKE

1 ⅓ cups graham cracker crumbs

¼ cup plus 1 tbsp butter

Three 8-oz packages cream cheese, at room temperature

1 ½ cup sugar, divided into 2 equal amounts

3 eggs

1 vanilla bean, or 1 tsp vanilla extract

1 cup blueberries

1 cup partridgeberries

1 tbsp cornstarch

Preheat oven to 350°F. Grease a 9-inch springform pan and line it with parchment paper. Mix graham cracker crumbs and butter and press into spring-form pan, forming the crust. Beat cream cheese and ¾ cup of sugar together in a large bowl for about 5 minutes. Add eggs one at a time to the mixture, letting the mixer run for about 2 minutes after each addition. Add vanilla and mix. Pour half of this mixture over the crust and let sit in the fridge while you make a quick jam.

Put berries in a pot with ¾ cup sugar over medium heat, and let the berries cook down for about 7 minutes. Make a cornstarch slurry by mixing the cornstarch with 1 tablespoon of water. Add that to your jam and cook for another 5 minutes while stirring, then take off the heat and let your jam cool. Once the cake is cool, take it out of the fridge and spread the jam in a thick layer over the cream cheese. Then top the jam with the remaining cream cheese mixture. Bake for 50 minutes, then remove and let cool. Once cooled, let sit in the fridge for 4 hours.

Brown Butter Damson Cake | page 169

Brown Butter Damson Cake

MAKES ONE 9-INCH CAKE

Damsons are a subspecies of plum. They are packed full of puckery sour and sweet flavour and they sing with browned butter. Poppy seeds would be a beautiful addition to this cake.

8 tbsp butter

1 ½ cups all-purpose flour

1 ½ tsp baking powder

1 tsp cinnamon

¼ tsp nutmeg

⅛ tsp cardamom

½ tsp salt

1 cup plus 2 tbsp sugar

1 large egg

1 tsp vanilla extract

½ cup buttermilk

1 cup damson plums, pitted and halved

Preheat oven to 350°F. Grease a 9-inch springform pan and line with parchment paper. Begin by browning the butter. Melt it over medium heat and let it turn a gorgeous nutty brown, then let it cool at room temperature for about 20 minutes. Whisk together the flour, baking powder, cinnamon, nutmeg, cardamom, and salt. In the bowl of an electric mixer fitted with the paddle attachment or beaters, cream the butter and 1 cup of sugar until pale and fluffy. I like to let this go for about 5 minutes. Now, beat in the egg and add vanilla. Finally, gently mix in your dry ingredients, alternating with the buttermilk. **NOTE: _Don't overmix or the cake will get tough._** Transfer the batter to the prepared pan and smooth the top with an offset spatula. Finally, arrange your plums in a beautiful circle. Bake for 60 to 70 minutes, until golden on top and set in the centre. I like this for breakfast with a shot of espresso.

Beer Bread Recipe   **MAKES 1 LOAF**

This is my version of a Newfoundland beer bread. I like to toss in dried serviceberries instead of raisins, and pumpkin seeds for crunch, and I prefer to use a local porter!

2 tbsp melted butter

2 ¾ cup flour

1 tbsp baking powder

1 ½ tsp salt

Handful of dried serviceberries (optional)

⅓ cup pumpkin seeds, toasted

One 10-oz can porter or stout

¼ cup honey

Preheat oven to 350°F. Grease a loaf pan with one tablespoon of the melted butter. Combine the flour, baking powder, salt, dried serviceberries, and half of your toasted pumpkin seeds in one bowl. The rest will be a garnish. Pour in your beer and honey and mix until it just comes together. **NOTE: _No kneading necessary!_** Pour the batter into the prepared pan and pour the remaining tablespoon of butter over the batter. Sprinkle the pumpkin seeds onto the top of the loaf and bake for 40 minutes. This goes well with just about any soup.

APPLES

Okay, foraging apples in Newfoundland is one of my favourite things. There are so many beautiful wild apple trees within walking distance from my house. They are everywhere. My top-secret spots must remain top secret, but I'm sure a short drive out of town in September will lead you to yours. Apples are abundant here. Pick your apples carefully, following the foraging rules outlined in previous chapters. Wash them well and look for worms. PEI apples are covered in slugs and worms, but I've had terrific luck with wild Newfoundland apples. Occasionally one or two will be blemished or wormy but mostly they are beautiful and tart.

I found this amazing apple recipe in a recipe book that someone had donated to The Rooms Provincial Archives. The book itself is full of little handwritten notes, newspaper clippings, and lists. The following recipe was clipped from one of the local newspapers in 1934, but I couldn't figure out which paper. Regardless, the recipe was brilliant and simple.

Breakfast Apples

This is a good way of taking your morning apples. Peel and core the required number. Fill the centers with cooked pork sausage. Bake for fifteen minutes in a good oven and serve on crisp fried bread.

Breakfast Apples 2.0

MAKES ENOUGH FOR 2 LARGE OR 4 SMALLER SERVINGS

1 tbsp olive oil

1 small onion, chopped

1 tbsp fresh rosemary, chopped

2 ¼ cups minced pork

1 apple, grated

2 cloves garlic, chopped small

1 egg

½ tsp smoked paprika

¼ cup smoked cheddar

Heat oil over medium-high heat in a medium-sized pan. Sauté the onions until golden brown, 5 to 7 minutes. Combine rosemary, pork, apple, chopped garlic, onions, egg, paprika, and cheddar in a mixing bowl. Form four thinnish patties, about half an inch thick.

TIP > You can also make and freeze some for later or cook them in batches.

At this stage, I usually put another splash of oil in my pan and cook these like burgers on medium heat, about 7 minutes per side.

I eat this on a bagel with greens, hot sauce, more cheese, and maybe bacon.

Apple Crumble Pie

MAKES ONE 9-INCH PIE

There's a lot of pie in this book, but this crumble pie made with wild apples is a favourite. You can peel your foraged apples or leave the peel on—it's full of flavour and fibre.

1 pie crust (see recipe on page 114)

6 cups cored and diced apples

2 tsp lemon juice

1 cup brown sugar, lightly packed

1 tsp ground cinnamon

1 tsp ground cardamom

½ cup unsalted butter, softened

½ cup flour

½ cup quick oats

¼ cup large flake oats

1 tsp salt

Handful pecans or walnuts (optional)

Prepare pie crust and let cool completely.

Preheat oven to 375°F. Mix lemon juice with apples as soon as they are diced to prevent discoloration, then mix your gorgeous lemony apples with half a cup of the brown sugar and the cinnamon and cardamom.

Mix the remaining half-cup of sugar with softened butter, flour, quick oats, large flake oats, and salt; throw in your nuts too, if you're using them. Place the apples in the pie crust and cover them with the crumble. Bake for 50 minutes.

PUMPKINS

Pumpkins are one of autumn's best treats. Oh sure, the wool sweaters, crisp air, and beautiful scenery are all great, but I think pumpkins are the best part of the season. All the local bakeries and cafés get in on the act with seasonal pumpkin spice treats, but I burn out on muffins and scones pretty quickly, so in my archival adventures I found some cool seasonal recipes and adapted them.

First, a little trivia about pumpkins. 1 > most pumpkins are edible, and 2 > pumpkins are not vegetables; they are actually berries—a fact that kind of blew my mind!

Here's a quick primer on the best eating pumpkins.

JACK-O'-LANTERN PUMPKINS For a long time, I thought the orange jack-o'-lantern pumpkins were too stringy to be of much use in the kitchen. Not so! Those orange globes make beautiful soups and curries. Pick a smaller one. There will be less water and more sugar, so the flesh will be sweeter. I use this variety for more savoury dishes.

SUGAR PUMPKINS These are the best for baking projects. The texture is incredibly smooth, which is great for pies and cakes. I also roast these for soup, and I treat them exactly as you would treat a butternut squash. They work when boiled and steamed, but roasted is the best way to bring out that caramel flavour. I also love these for a vegan Thanksgiving idea. I scoop out the sides, leaving the pumpkin shape intact. I cut the flesh into 1-inch pieces, toss it with olive oil and spices, then roast in the oven. Mix those roasted pumpkin pieces with wild rice, toasted pecans, dried cherries, herbs, pomegranate, and a little lemon juice and olive oil. Stuff it into the sugar pumpkin bowl for a real showstopper that will make the turkey-eaters a little jealous.

FAIRY-TALE PUMPKINS These green magical-looking orbs are especially high in beta-carotene, which our bodies turn into vitamin A. They have the sweetest flavour and I like them with gnocchi, browned butter, sage, and a little Parmesan.

CANNED PUMPKIN PURÉE I actually can't get enough of canned pumpkin purée. The texture is unbeatable and my pumpkin pies always turn out perfectly! Purée isn't to be confused with canned pumpkin pie filling—that is obscenely sugary and contains a god-awful amount of preservatives. Canned purée usually has no additives. I always end up with some purée left over, so I tend to fold it into waffle and pancake batter.

This old recipe doesn't make a ton of sense. It doesn't give us a serving size. There's a lot of information that we're lacking, so I adjusted it and added ginger for the 2.0 version.

Old-School Pumpkin Marmalade

8 cups pumpkin

7 cups sugar

3 oranges

1 lemon

1 grapefruit

1/2 tsp salt

Peel, seed, and dice pumpkin into 1/2-inch cubes. Squeeze juice from fruit, mince half of peel from each fruit and add all together in the bowl. Add sugar and salt. Let stand overnight. In the morning, put into a bottle and bring to a boil, turn down the heat and simmer for 1 1/2 hours. Pour into hot bottles. Seal.

Pumpkin Ginger Marmalade 2.0

MAKES ENOUGH TO FILL 1 SMALL MASON JAR

As always, I tried to keep the recipe size small, so little goes to waste if you don't enjoy it. I've adapted this recipe by decreasing the sugar content, adding vanilla and ginger, and playing with the ratios.

2 small sugar pie pumpkins

1 tbsp olive oil

¾ cups white or brown sugar

1 tbsp fresh orange juice

½ tbsp lemon juice

1 tbsp grated fresh ginger

Pinch salt

½ tsp pure vanilla extract

Preheat oven to 350°F and line a baking sheet with parchment paper. Use a sharp chef's knife to cut your pumpkins in half. Remove the top and bottom of the pumpkin. Scoop out all the seeds and stringy parts in the middle with a spoon. Brush your pumpkins with a tablespoon of olive oil. Place flesh-side down on the baking sheet and pierce the skin a few times to let steam escape. Bake for about 45 minutes, or until the pumpkin flesh is nice and soft. You can peel your pumpkin once it's cooled, but the skin contains fibre and flavour, so you can also leave it.

Once your pumpkin is cooled, purée it in a food process until perfectly smooth. Put the purée in a heavy-duty saucepan along with the sugar, orange juice, lemon juice, ginger, salt, and vanilla. Cook over a low-medium heat. Stir constantly to prevent the purée from burning, for about 10 minutes. **NOTE: *The marmalade should be nice and thick.*** Take off the heat and let it cool. Scrape into a clean jar. It's beautiful on toast and keeps for a month in the fridge.

Homemade Iced Pumpkin Coffee

MAKES ENOUGH SYRUP FOR 8 CUPS OF COFFEE

for the syrup
1 cup water
¾ cup maple syrup
2 tbsp pumpkin marmalade (see recipe on page 176)
1 tsp ground cinnamon
½ tsp cardamom
¼ tsp ground nutmeg
¼ tsp ground cloves

MAKES 1 GLASS OF COFFEE

for the coffee
6 plain ice cubes or coffee ice cubes
1 cup cold coffee
2 tbsp pumpkin spice syrup
Cream, to taste

Okay, here's a shocker: there are no archived recipes for pumpkin spice coffee. Look, I know pumpkin spice lattes are annoying and everyone hates the things, but let's talk about how that particular flavour combination actually works beautifully. Cinnamon and nutmeg really sing with coffee. I think it's a beautiful combination, so here's a quick-and-easy iced pumpkin coffee that uses some of the marmalade from the recipe on page 176 to make a syrup to flavour the coffee.

to make the syrup
To make the pumpkin spice syrup, combine all ingredients in a small saucepan. Bring to a simmer over low-medium heat. Simmer for 20 minutes, stirring occasionally. Remove from heat; then let it cool to room temperature. Strain to remove solids. This syrup should keep for about a month in the fridge.

to make the coffee
Just add ice cubes and 2 tablespoons of pumpkin spice syrup to your chilled coffee.

Pumpkin Soup

Usually, when I make soup, I'm thinking about acidity, sweetness, texture, and heat. Soups need a hint of acidity to be truly balanced. To achieve this, I usually add lemon juice, lime juice, or apple cider vinegar. Other times, a soup will be too sour, and maple syrup, honey, or a little brown sugar is needed to square it out. I want some types of soup to be chunky, but others should be smooth. Finally, I find that a little heat really improves the fullness and mouth feel. Pumpkin soup is so naturally sweet that I don't end up adding any other sweet element. I add apples for acidity, and cayenne and paprika for heat. I think a nice smooth purée is the way to go here.

1 sugar pie pumpkin

4 tbsp olive oil

1 large onion, chopped

1 Honeycrisp apple, chopped but not peeled

1 tsp sea salt

½ tsp ground cinnamon

⅛ tsp ground cloves

Pinch cayenne pepper

½ tsp paprika

black pepper, freshly ground, to taste

6 medium cloves garlic, grated

4 cups vegetable broth

½ cup full-fat coconut milk (optional)

1 tbsp maple syrup

¼ cup pumpkin seeds (optional)

Sage (optional)

Goat's cheese (optional)

Preheat oven to 350°F and line a baking sheet with parchment paper. Use a sharp chef's knife to cut your pumpkins in half. Remove the top and bottom ends of the pumpkin. Scoop out all the seeds and stringy parts in the middle with a spoon. Brush your pumpkins with a tablespoon of olive oil. Place flesh-side down on the baking sheet and pierce the skin a few times to let steam escape. Bake for about 45 minutes, or until the pumpkin flesh is nice and soft.

NOTE: *You can peel your pumpkin once it's cooled, but the skin contains fibre and flavour, so you can also leave it.*

Heat the remaining 3 tablespoons of olive oil in a large Dutch oven or heavy-bottomed pot over medium heat. Once the oil is shimmering, add onion, chopped apple, salt, cinnamon, cloves, cayenne, paprika, and black pepper to the pot. Stir to combine. Cook, stirring occasionally, until onion is translucent, about 8 to 10 minutes. Add garlic.

Add the pumpkin flesh, more salt, and a few twists of the pepper grinder's worth of black pepper. Add broth, and bring to a boil, then reduce heat and simmer for 30 minutes. This is a great time to toast some pumpkin seeds and chop up some sage. Pumpkin also pairs well with goat's cheese, so you could prep that now, too.

Once the pumpkin mixture has finished cooking, stir in the coconut milk if using, and maple syrup. Remove the soup from heat and let it cool slightly. Serve with sage, crumbled goat's cheese, and toasted pumpkin seeds.

I made a grilled cheese sandwich to go with this and it was the best.

TIP > You can use an immersion blender to blend this soup in the pot.

COLCANNON NIGHT IN NEWFOUNDLAND

I found seven old recipes for colcannon in my archive adventures, and I was delighted each time. I've read about the dish in Irish cookbooks, but I had no idea that the Celtic tradition of eating colcannon on Halloween had once been alive and celebrated here. In fact, before the 1930s, Halloween in Newfoundland was commonly called Colcannon Night! This night had many of the same traditions and sprang from the same well as Halloween. It was a night of loud parties, superstitions, ancient beliefs, games, mischief, dancing, and sweet treats. Folks gathered for a meal of colcannon—usually root vegetables mashed with butter, mixed with onions, and sometimes meat. This varies from the Irish version in two ways: **1** the Irish dish almost always features kale and **2** The Irish dish consists solely of potatoes for root vegetable, while here in Newfoundland it would be made with turnip, parsnip, or whatever root vegetable was handy.

Both recipes involve hidden surprises, though this varied by region. In Newfoundland, each colcannon dish contained four objects: a ring, a coin, an old maid's thimble, and a bachelor's button (which, confusingly, is also a type of flower). The finder of the ring would marry soon, the finder of the coin would get rich, while the finders of the thimble and button would die alone and never marry. Bit of a bummer to get the last two! The St. John's newspaper the *Evening Telegram* reported on November 1, 1902, "Fortune-telling, scrying and other games were all part of the fun. The town was lively last night with parties. The young folks were entertained with snap apple, while older ones enjoyed themselves at the altar of Terpsichore, the clear cold air resounding to the musical strains till early morning."

I really love this quote; it sent me down a beautiful Halloween rabbit-hole. First, I had to figure out what snap apple was. Turns out, it's a pretty intense game that used to be played on October 31. Two pieces of wood were tied together to form a cross, which was then hung horizontally from a tree or door. Two candles were jabbed into the ends of two of the sticks, and apples into the other two ends.

The candles were lit and someone would set the whole thing spinning. Daring folks would try to take a bite of an apple without getting burned. In later evolutions of the game, it seems like the apples were simply hung from doorframes and sent spinning.

Most recipes for colcannon were pretty simple and laid out as follows:

`Wash and cook vegetables. Put through a potato ricer. Mix well and heat in a saucepan with butter for added flavour. Serve hot.`

My version of colcannon is vegan!

Colcannon 2.0

MAKES ENOUGH FOR 4 TO 6 PEOPLE

5 cups peeled sweet potatoes, cut into quarters

1 ¼ tsp kosher salt

⅓ cup full-fat coconut milk

3 tbsp olive oil

2 celery stalks, chopped into semicircles

3 cloves garlic, minced

Salt, to taste

4 cups chopped kale leaves, stems removed

4 green onions, finely chopped

⅓ cup water

2 tbsp nutritional yeast

¼ tsp black pepper

Vegan "butter" spread, such as Earth Balance, for serving

Boil the sweet potatoes. Once they're cooked, drain and mash them with salt and coconut milk. Put two tablespoons of oil in pan on medium heat. Add the celery to the pan and cook for about 5 minutes. Add garlic and cook for 1 minute. Add a little salt, kale, and most of the green onions, reserving a teaspoonful or two for garnish, and the remaining tablespoon of oil. Cook for about 4 minutes, stirring occasionally. Once the kale looks a little crispy and cooked, add the water and let cook for about 3 minutes. Take the vegetables off the heat and stir them into the mashed sweet potato. Finally, add nutritional yeast, black pepper, a little more salt to taste, and a garnish of green onion.

You can spread some butter-substitute on top, but it's tasty on its own.

FALL MUSHROOM FORAGING

Hunting for mushrooms is a special part of living in modern Newfoundland, but it isn't a traditional activity. While Newfoundlanders have eaten dandelion salads and engaged in a variety of other early spring foraging, wild mushrooms were avoided as they were considered poisonous. Consequently, early settlers really missed out, because our mushrooms are amazing—nutty and peppery, fragrant and flavourful. I like them best with garlic and freshly grated Parmesan, and tend to spend the season folding them into pastas and quiches.

I should also state that I'm not a mushroom expert, just a passionate enthusiast. As such, I tend to hunt and pick only hedgehog mushrooms, golden chanterelles, winter chanterelles, and the occasional bolete—mushrooms that I can easily identify. I buy the rest from my favourite forager—Shawn Dawson of the Barking Kettle.

If you're heading into the woods, here are a few tips for the hunt.

1 Identify correctly.

The first rule of mushroom hunting is a bit obvious, but correct identification is key! The golden chanterelle shares the forest with look-alikes, and they can cause extreme gastric discomfort. There are dozens of poisonous mushrooms on the Avalon, so if you're interested in mushroom hunting, understand that it's a subject you should learn patiently. Gain experience by attending a mushroom foray with an expert, take a walk with a forager, buy some books, attend lectures, and **don't pick to eat or share until you're positive the mushroom is safe to eat**. There's an old saying, "There are old mushroom hunters, there are bold mushroom hunters, but there are no old, bold mushroom hunters."

2 Keep your patch a secret.

The second rule of mushroom hunting is we don't talk about mushroom hunting! More specifically, don't tell people where your patch is. Chanterelle patches are old and very slow to reproduce, so if there's evidence that someone else is harvesting from a particular patch, move on. The biggest threat to a patch is damage from trampling, which damages the mycelium—the roots of the organism we see as a mushroom.

3 Don't pick all the baby chanterelles. Resist temptation.

The third rule is to leave some or most of the small chanterelles in the ground. Yes, they taste delicious and yes, you're excited that the season has begun, but harvesting an entire patch of baby chanterelles is a bad idea. Mushrooms themselves are the reproductive parts of the organism, so baby chanterelles, if harvested, won't have a chance to release spores and propagate new mushrooms.

4 Leave some for the other animals.

Mushrooms are an important source of nutrients for almost every living thing in the bogs and barrens of Newfoundland. Don't pick a patch clean.

5 Only pick what you'll use.

There are lots of folks who go mushroom hunting, filling garbage bags with these gorgeous golden treats. I've stumbled on folks taking selfies with their mushrooms before discarding the entire lot they've just picked. This makes me angry. Hunting for chanterelles isn't something that someone should do just "for the 'gram." Unless you're a professional forager, you should pick only what you'll actually use. For me, I'm happy with a few pints to pickle and a handful here and there for quiches, scrambled eggs, and soups. Speaking of which . . .

Chanterelle Soup

MAKES ENOUGH FOR 4 PEOPLE

1 lb chanterelles, cleaned

3 tbsp butter

½ Spanish onion, finely chopped

¼ cup parsley, chopped

½ cup dill, chopped

Salt and pepper, to taste

2 tbsp flour (optional)

3 cups vegetable broth

½ cup heavy cream or ¼ cup sherry

Grated Parmesan, for garnish (optional)

NOTE: *Pick over the chanterelles and give them a good cleaning with a mushroom brush—a pastry brush will do in a pinch. I don't recommend washing chanterelles in water. They tend to lose flavour, go limp, and just become less appealing. A little forest debris won't hurt you!*

Once your chanterelles are cleaned, chop them finely. Next, melt the butter in a saucepan over medium heat; add the mushrooms, onion, parsley, and dill. After several minutes of sautéing, salt your mushrooms and onions!

TIP > Lots of people will just season their soups at the end, but you want to layer your seasoning.

Sauté everything until the moisture released by the mushrooms evaporates. This will take about 10 minutes. Sprinkle in the flour. Stir for another few minutes and then add the broth gradually, whisking as you go. Raise the heat to a boil and once it's reached, lower the heat to a simmer for 20 minutes. Stir in the cream or sherry, taking care not to let the soup boil again.

Purée the whole thing in a blender. Season with salt and pepper. Shave some fresh Parmesan onto the top of the soup as a garnish. I also like to garnish with a few leftover sautéed chanterelles and some more dill and parsley. Enjoy!

NOTE: *Garlic is a beautiful addition to this soup, especially when roasted! Just purée it into the soup. This is an incredibly rich soup, so a small portion goes a long way. I make a vegan version with coconut oil instead of butter and coconut milk instead of cream. I like to add navy beans into the mix before I purée, it for added protein and improved texture!*

Chanterelle Toast for One

MAKES ENOUGH FOR 1 PERSON

1 medium slice good sourdough bread

3 tbsp butter, softened

1 clove garlic

2 handfuls chanterelles, cleaned and dried

1 tsp lemon juice

1 tsp chopped flat leaf parsley

1 tbsp grated Parmesan

Toast the bread, spread one tablespoon of softened butter all over it, and let it melt into the nooks and crannies of the bread. Rub the clove of garlic over the buttered surface of the toast. Chop your mushrooms until they are the desired size. I like chanterelles to retain most of their shape, so I just slice up the big ones.

Next, chop the garlic up and set it aside. Heat the frying pan—preferably a good cast-iron one—over medium-high heat, and when it's hot, add a tablespoon of butter. Once the butter is hot, add the chanterelles. Cook for 4 minutes without moving them around too much; let them soak up the butter. Add the lemon juice and remaining tablespoon of butter. Let the mushrooms absorb this liquid; it should take 4 to 5 more minutes. **NOTE:** *Don't worry about the butter burning; it may darken, but the browning should just add delicious flavour.*

Toss the garlic into the pan and stir it into the mushrooms. After a minute, spoon mushrooms out onto the toast. Sprinkle the whole thing with chopped parsley and Parmesan. Enjoy!

Easy Chanterelle Pasta

MAKES ENOUGH FOR 4 PEOPLE

4 cups dry or fresh pasta

1 cup chanterelle mushrooms, cleaned

2 tbsp olive oil

½ medium onion, chopped

7 cloves garlic, minced

½ tsp salt, or to taste

½ tsp pepper, or to taste

½ cup white wine

¼ cup parsley, chopped

1 cup grated Parmesan cheese

¼ cup grated aged cheddar

Pine nuts, basil, and borage to garnish

Cook your pasta according to the instructions on the package. For this recipe, I used some pasta from a local maker, and I recommend that if possible. Reserve a cup of the pasta water and remember that for pasta to really sing, the water you boil the pasta in should taste like the sea, so add a ton of salt to the cooking water. Drain your pasta when cooked, and set aside.

Slice your cleaned mushrooms in half or quarters. I also sometimes like to leave the small ones whole because they look so pretty. Sauté your onions in the olive oil, on medium heat. Let this go for about 5 minutes, then add your chopped garlic and mushrooms. Let this sauté for a little while. Season with salt and pepper, add the wine and let that simmer off for about 5 minutes.

Add the pasta back into the pan and add half a cup of pasta water. Add the parsley, Parmesan, and cheddar, and let this thicken a bit, about 5 minutes.

TIP > Pasta water contains starch and is a key to making a quick sauce. If things get a bit too thick, you can add that last half-cup of pasta water.

Garnish with pine nuts, basil, and borage leaves. Top with more Parmesan and enjoy! You can also serve this pasta with pesto, or just butter.

Hedgehog and Winter Chanterelle Mushroom Ramen

for the broth

¼ cup vegetable oil

4 cups hedgehog mushrooms, cleaned and chopped

1 cup winter chanterelles, cleaned

Pinch salt

1 onion, chopped

4 cloves garlic, chopped

1 cup dry white wine

½ cup soy sauce

½ tsp dried lemon thyme

½ tsp fresh rosemary, finely chopped

5 cups water

1 tbsp white miso paste

for the noodles

1 tbsp vegetable oil

1 tbsp chopped garlic

1 tbsp grated ginger

1 cup hedgehog mushrooms, cleaned

Two 3-oz packages ramen noodles

1 tbsp rice wine vinegar

1 carrot, grated

4 large eggs, soft-boiled

2 green onions, chopped

Crushed peanuts (optional)

Hot sauce (optional)

MAKES ENOUGH FOR 4 HUNGRY PEOPLE

Ramen can be really intimidating for folks, so we're starting nice and easy here. This isn't a recipe where I tell you to make homemade noodles! We'll get a rich broth going and the rest will be pretty easy and painless.

to make the broth

In a cast-iron pan or large Dutch oven, heat the vegetable oil over medium-high heat. Next, sauté the mushrooms in batches of about 2 handfuls at a time.

NOTE: *Overcrowding the pan is a big no-no: the mushrooms will be undercooked and unappealing, and won't release the umami that we want in our broth.*

Stir for about 5 minutes until the mushrooms release their liquid, and then season with salt. After each batch, remove the mushrooms and place in a separate bowl. Once the mushrooms are done, drizzle a little more vegetable oil into the pan, toss in the onion, and cook until translucent. Add the garlic and cook for a minute, then season again. Add the wine, soy sauce, thyme, rosemary, water, and white miso paste. Throw the cooked mushrooms back into the pot and bring to a boil. Reduce the heat to medium low, cover, and let simmer for 1 hour. Strain out all the solids. Then strain again! You should be left with about 3 cups of mushroom broth. You're ready to make some delicious mushroom ramen. Also, if you have extra, the broth freezes beautifully.

continued on page 194

to make the noodles

Heat vegetable oil in a large stockpot or Dutch oven over medium heat. Add garlic and ginger and cook for about 2 minutes, stirring frequently, until fragrant. Stir in hedgehog mushrooms and sauté for about 5 minutes until golden brown. Add homemade broth, then ramen noodles. Stir for about 3 minutes, until ramen is just tender. Stir in rice wine vinegar; season with additional soy sauce and pepper, to taste.

Garnish with carrots, eggs, green onions. I also like to top mine with crushed peanuts and hot sauce.

Cream of Hedgehog Mushroom Soup

MAKES ENOUGH FOR 4 PEOPLE

Hedgehog mushrooms make an excellent soup, but you need to get over the hurdle that is the really unappetizing colour. I fooled around with this recipe to try and make it more appealing to look at, without success. To really enjoy the gorgeous hedgehog flavour, you just need to make do with the pale milky colour. Accept that this soup is ugly, and enjoy.

¼ cup olive oil, more as needed

1 medium onion, chopped

2 large cloves garlic

6 cups hedgehog or chanterelle mushrooms, cleaned and roughly chopped

6 cups mushroom stock

Salt and pepper, to taste

⅓ cup port

Handful walnuts, toasted (optional)

Truffle oil (optional)

Fresh rosemary, chopped (optional)

Heat your oil in a pan on medium heat. Toss in the chopped onions and let them get nice and translucent. After 5 minutes, add in the garlic and let it toast for a minute. Toss the mushrooms into the mix and let those cook for about 7 to 10 minutes. **NOTE:** *They should get a little caramelized and will release all of their delicious liquid.* Remember to stir them from time to time.

TIP > When they're ready, you can take some of these mushrooms out and reserve them as a garnish, or just leave them all in.

Add the stock and bring to a boil, then lower the heat and cook for a good 30 minutes. Adjust the seasoning and, at the very end, stir in your port. Remove soup from the heat and purée.

I like to garnish this with toasted walnuts, truffle oil, and a little dusting of fresh rosemary.

FOREST GAME

The first thing I really take in is the cat on the leash. Daniel is holding up a gorgeous fluffy grey puss, the kind of cat that could have its own Instagram account—a real stunner. He's explaining his cat has some leashed yard time every day. The indoor/outdoor cat debate could fill a whole book. Cats who are allowed to roam have shorter lifespans and a very negative effect on the local songbird population. Other folks claim cats are predators who don't get to satisfy their natural curiosity when trapped indoors. Putting a cat on a leash for an hour or two per day seems to give cats the best of both worlds; they get to spend time outdoors in the natural world, but are prevented from wreaking havoc on the ecosystem. I'm not a vet, biologist, or cat owner, but I always interpret a cat on a leash as a good sign.

You see, Daniel Schoonhoven is a friend of a friend, and he's offered to take me hunting. I'm a little nervous about it. I've wanted to write about hunting for some time, but didn't know how to start. The debates surrounding the topic are complicated; some argue hunting is unnecessary in a culture capable of farming animals, while others suggest it's cruel and promotes gun acceptance in society. Perhaps the most compelling argument about hunting is the belief that it should be reserved solely for Indigenous communities. I've seen this argument surface on Twitter time and time again, and it always strikes a chord with me. While I'd like to see this idea explored, I'm not sure it's a story that should come from me.

There are counterpoints to the arguments listed above. First, hunting can be an effective form of animal population control. In places where there are no natural predators, animal populations can grow and grow to the point where they destroy ecosystems, causing large numbers to starve. Similarly, the hunters I've met tend to be great conservationists—using all parts of the animal and donating widely to conservation causes. Daniel agrees. "I think the more time someone spends in a natural environment, the greater the sense of appreciation and urge to preserve and protect that beauty." He points out that some of the world's most successful conservation efforts were founded by hunters, Ducks Unlimited being one of the best examples.

I should also stress that despite the debates, I've wanted to learn more about hunting for some time. Not trophy hunting—I have no interest in mounting heads. Instead, I'm interested in hunting small game, such as grouse, duck, and geese.

I love the flavour of game meat; it's rich and interesting and complex.

I've also made the decision that if I'm going to eat meat, it has to be locally farmed or game. I want to be involved in the way I eat and, to me, that means at least learning something basic about hunting.

Daniel and I climb into his jeep. He's taking me to a spot just outside town. On the way, he talks about gear. "A gun with a case, trigger lock, ammunition, and cleaning kit, some rubber boots, an article or two of bright orange clothing, and a sharp knife are what I'd consider the bare essentials." He glances down at my sneakers and says, "Maybe rubber boots are the most important thing." I nod and tell him that I am prepared to sacrifice my sneakers. Daniel has also packed extra layers of clothing, a wilderness survival kit, a variety of snacks, binoculars, and plastic bags for dressing game.

We're going hunting for ducks. It's later in the afternoon, and Daniel explains that we're going to trek around two ponds. The ducks land on the water around sunset to rest overnight. You're only allowed to hunt for thirty minutes after the sun has set—any later and it's far too dark to safely use a gun. Also, he warns me we're probably not going to get anything. "You tend to have much better luck earlier in the season," he says, "After that, they get a bit wary." We chat for a minute about how hunting can seem a little inaccessible. I've often felt that if you weren't born into a family of hunters, it can look impossible to learn. He agrees, but points out that the paperwork is very easy to take care of. "You are required to take the Canadian Firearms Safety Course and the Hunter Education Course in order to become eligible to hunt game with a firearm, but besides the courses, there is very little paperwork involved. You just need to provide basic information and certifications, and at the end of the season you submit information about what you harvested and observed. That data is used to aid in wildlife management."

I wonder aloud if the gear and the expense of starting up make it hard to get involved. "Not really" is Daniel's answer. "It could be hard to know where to start, but a shop like Outdoor Pros in Mount Pearl could help you get set up for just a few hundred dollars, which isn't any more expensive than getting into golf or skiing."

As we walk through the woods, a small wooden structure catches my eye. It's a duck blind built by other hunters. It looks like a fort you'd build in the woods as a kid—a little rickety, a little cozy. Ahead of us, three little ducks are floating on the water. Daniel signals us to stop, but then he says, "No. Those are just decoys."

We reverse and trek back the other way. Daniel's actually not great at shooting ducks; he's fairly new to it, and he's sharing stories about his near misses. He has better luck with partridge. "Oh! It's like woods chicken, but it's more comparable to a free-range chicken than a factory-farmed one." When he cooks game, he keeps it fairly simple so as to bring out the nice, subtle flavours. "A few days ago, I put the whole partridge breast along with some chunked vegetables in a casserole dish, I used some olive oil, sprinkled over a herb-based spice blend, poured a half-cup of wine in the bottom for moisture, and roasted it in the oven."

I'm particularly curious about gizzards. I've always wanted to confit them in duck fat and see if they taste as rich as I imagine. Daniel doesn't believe in wasting anything, but he doesn't touch gizzard anymore. "I'm a little burnt out on gizzards, but I don't waste them. I give it to a friend and he fries it up." We're almost definitely scaring away birds by chatting, but I have a lot of questions. I ask about field dressing and how quickly you need to break the animal down. "I field dress the animal as extensively as possible. It is very important to cool the meat ASAP. Field dressing immediately helps with that."

We're almost at our second spot now and the sun is setting. Small trees and tall reeds create a natural duck blind, and Daniel advises me to tuck inside and hide. "Ducks actually have incredible eyesight, so hiding and wearing camouflage is important." It's a little chilly and I am regretting the whole sneaker thing. Daniel

mentions that a lot of hunting is sitting and waiting. "Do you bring a book?" I ask. "No. I think the second you got absorbed into your book, the ducks would come and you'd miss your chance. You just sit and wait." I'm really impressed by this.

I feel as though—and this is just conjecture—hunting would probably help with your sense of concentration and focus. Daniel agrees. "Yeah, and it's really interesting what you can hear when there are no cars. No human noises. It's really peaceful."

The sun is setting, so we start waiting. Nothing comes. I think I see a duck out of the corner of my eye on the other side of the pond. I borrow Daniel's binoculars to investigate, but it's just a rock. A few minutes later I think I see a duck again, but it's just a bigger rock. We hear a bird call out and I look to Daniel hopefully, but no luck. "It's just a songbird." He tells me about a moose trip he recently undertook. His friend brought his sons and they all walked around the woods starting at 6 a.m., finding nothing. After getting back to the campsite, Daniel had a little nap in the sun and started snoring. The youngest boy was convinced the noises were coming from a moose in the woods and kept telling their father he could hear one. "His dad had to keep telling him that it was just me. It's funny, but when you're hunting you do start thinking every noise is the thing you want it to be."

Daniel calls it an evening on our behalf. It's 30 minutes after sunset. We're not getting a duck. I'm cold and a little desperate to warm my feet, but I'm not disappointed. I still had an adventure in the woods—on a weekday. As we head back to the jeep, I ask Daniel if he wants to respond to any misconceptions around hunting or hunters. "I think the big thing is debunking the idea that hunting is unethical or cruel. From a sustainability perspective, wild meat grows in harmony with the natural environment. There're no fertilizers or pesticides, and you don't get the ecological damage of macro-scale land clearing. I also think hunters, fishermen, and gatherers spend so much time outdoors that we end up having balanced perspectives on conservation. We understand that sustainability and conservation are less likely to succeed with no human interaction, but controlled human interaction is important."

Grouse Tenders

MAKES ENOUGH FOR 2 PEOPLE

1 grouse breast

1 large egg

2 tbsp buttermilk

⅓ cup flour

1 cup crackers, crushed

Vegetable oil to coat a pan

Rinse the breast and dry with paper towel, then cut into strips. Whisk the egg and buttermilk together in a shallow bowl. Put the flour in a separate bowl. Fill a third bowl with crushed crackers—the homemade cracker recipe on page 37 would work beautifully for this. Now dip the grouse strips first in the flour, then the egg, and finally the crushed crackers. Heat the vegetable oil in a cast-iron pan on medium heat. Fry strips until golden brown and then place on paper towels.

Braised Rabbit Stew 2.0

MAKES ENOUGH FOR 2 TO 4 PEOPLE

Rabbit recipes are not scarce on the ground. Usually, they call for turnips, carrots, potatoes, and a pastry topping. I'm down with all of that, but I think braising and marinating the rabbit makes a big difference. My mother-in-law gave me two skinned and cleaned rabbits last year for Christmas. I was thrilled. What's a better gift than delicious rabbit flavour, with absolutely none of the work? Call me easy to please, but it was one of the best gifts I've ever received. Rabbit has a bad reputation. Folks like to complain about the toughness of the meat and the grey, unappetizing colour, but I think rabbit can be wonderful and rewarding— you just need to treat it right. Also, it deserves and needs good accompaniments. I like it with crusty bread and a red wine that lives just outside what I can afford. Here's a braised stew that does rabbit justice.

for the marinade
1 cup red wine

8 cloves garlic, grated

2 sprigs rosemary

Herb sachet of dried alder or dried Labrador tea

2 tsp salt

to make the marinade
Mix all of the ingredients together, pour into a pot, place your rabbit inside, and marinate overnight in the fridge.

to make the stew
Remove the rabbit from the marinade and discard the marinade. Pat the rabbit dry and season with salt and pepper. Seasoning is a personal thing, but use a bit more salt than you would normally. Toss the rabbit pieces in a bowl with the flour, making sure to coat them evenly. Heat the oil in a large, deep cast-iron pan or Dutch oven on medium-high heat. Working in batches,

for the stew

¼ cup vegetable oil

1 rabbit, broken into pieces

Salt and pepper, to taste

¼ cup flour

1 large onion, chopped

3 carrots, chopped into small pieces

2 celery stalks, chopped into small, even pieces

6 cloves garlic, grated

¼ cup dry red wine

1 cup chicken broth

1 cup tomato sauce or purée

1 bay leaf

1 tbsp fresh rosemary or oregano, chopped

½ cup barley (optional)

sear all of your rabbit pieces. Give them a nice even browning and a good crust. The rabbit should sizzle when it hits the pan, and each piece should take about 3 minutes. Remove the meat and set aside.

Add onions, carrot, and celery to the pan. Let those brown for about 5 minutes, then toss in the garlic. **NOTE:** *Garlic burns quickly, so only give it a minute on the heat.* Next, deglaze the pan using a dry red wine—boxed wine will do! Save your good wines for drinking. Use a spoon to scrape all the delicious brown bits off the bottom. Don't toss those brown bits, just get them loose. Return the meat to the pot, then add the chicken broth and tomato sauce. Add a little water—not much, half a cup at the most. Bring to a boil. Add the bay leaf, cover, and simmer for about 45 minutes.

Once that's done, remove the rabbit from the pot and pick the meat off the bones. Put the meat back in the pot, add the herbs, and the barley if using it. Cook for another 40 minutes at low heat. **NOTE:** *Your stew should be thick, red, and delicious.*

Serve with a Pinot noir, and maybe a green leafy salad to cut through the richness and stave off gout, and bread or biscuits for dunking.

Christmas

STIR-UP SUNDAY

November can be a tough month. The beauty of fall has faded, but you aren't quite ready to deck the halls. That's why I make a point of celebrating "Stir-Up Sunday." Stir-Up Sunday is an old English/Welsh tradition that some Newfoundlanders still subscribe to. Haven't heard of it? I'm hardly shocked. Even in its countries of origin, fewer and fewer young people know about it. In the last few centuries, the final Sunday before Advent (usually the last of November) has been celebrated by home cooks who "stir up" their Christmas cakes and puddings. The name has often been traced to the prayer said on that day in the Anglican Church, "Stir up, we beseech thee, O Lord, the wills of thy faithful people."

Stir-Up Sunday enjoyed its heyday during Queen Victoria's reign, but its roots lie in feudal times. Medieval cooks celebrated the holiday by making frumenty, a type of oatmeal or porridge dish studded with grains, dried fruit, and spices before being "stirred" into a savoury meat broth. Ale and spirits were added as Christmas approached. This would have tasted awful, but it was the Middle Ages so we'll cut them some slack. Here in Newfoundland, Stir-Up Sunday is still celebrated by pockets of people in different bays and inlets. An article published in Spaniard's Bay in the 1950s argued that Stir-Up Sunday was important because it challenged apathy, reminding us to slow down and to not take things for granted. I can get behind that idea; it's a good reason to take a day and put it aside for holiday baking. However, if the aim of the tradition is to be mindful and grateful, then why is it vanishing?

Well, that's complicated. We can probably begin by blaming the convenient foods that feed our busier lives. We move faster than before, squeezing activities, meetings, and Snapchats into every minute. To deal with our lack of time, contemporary holidays involve pre-stuffed turkeys and those Robin Hood–brand boxes of Nanaimo bar mix. There's no shame in the boxed cake game, but it is a far cry from devoting an entire day to a Christmas pudding. On a similar note, it was and is a privilege to go to great lengths just to have something sweet for the holidays. Lower-income families, families new to Canada, and single-parent families would have skipped the tradition because there was more important work to be done.

Like many food traditions, Stir-Up Sunday is all tangled up with privilege and wealth. I think we need to bring it back. Not in its old-fashioned form—I'm not advocating for women to spend the day making pudding while the men chop wood or go fishing. Traditions are living things that need to evolve. I'm suggesting that you take the day and bake something. Take that time to think about the privileges you experience and to really appreciate how lucky you are to be able to make something from scratch.

Traditionally, Stir-Up Sunday puddings involved thirteen ingredients, one each for Jesus and his twelve disciples. If you want to follow that old rule, I've included a recipe. But if you want to toss it out, I've also included a Christmas cake recipe with just five ingredients. Also, if you come from a culture that does not relish Christmas cake or acknowledge the Advent calendar in any way, bake something that's special to you. It's the spirit of the tradition (feeling grateful and taking time) that we need to hold on to, not the rules.

Christmas Cake 2.0

MAKES 1 BIG CAKE

If you're going to take part in Stir-Up Sunday, then I suggest this simple recipe; it makes a large quantity without much fuss.

6 cups dried mixed fruit

2 ½ cups orange juice

Splash dark rum or sherry

2 cups self-rising flour

Handful pecans for top of cake

Place the mixed dried fruit into a very large bowl. Add the orange juice and mix well. Add the splash of booze now too. I've suggested rum or sherry, but brandy or even an Irish cream will work well. Cover with plastic wrap and place in the fridge overnight.

Preheat oven to 350°F. Grease and line an 8-inch pan with parchment paper and set aside. Stir the self-rising flour through the fruit mixture, then pour it all into the prepared pan. Top with pecans and cover with tinfoil. This will keep the nuts from darkening too much. Bake for approximately 1 hour or until the cake feels firm in the middle and a skewer inserted comes out with a few moist crumbs on it. Let it sit for 24 hours. You can serve it now with a hard sauce, custard, or whipped cream, or you can poke holes in it and soak it every few days with rum or sherry, until Christmas. This cake freezes really well, too.

Old-School Stir-Up Sunday Figgy Pudding with 13 Ingredients

MAKES ENOUGH FOR 4 PEOPLE

This is the perfect Victorian-era recipe for Christmas. A figgy pudding is a lot more like a soufflé than a fruitcake. Traditionally, figgy puddings were made with walnuts, but I've replaced them with pecans because I think walnuts become a little bitter once wet, and you're going to want to soak this whole thing in brandy or rum. This recipe freezes well, so you can make it on any free afternoon and jam it in the deep freeze until the holidays. You can soak it in rum overnight and serve with whipped cream on Christmas Day.

½ cup butter, at room temperature

2 large eggs

1 cup molasses

2 cups dried figs, stems removed, chopped fine

½ tsp lemon peel, grated

1 cup buttermilk

½ cup pecans, chopped

2 ½ cups all-purpose flour

½ tsp baking soda

2 tsp baking powder

1 tsp salt

1 tsp ground cinnamon

Pinch ground cardamom

Preheat oven to 325°F. Grease and flour an 8×4-inch soufflé dish. In an electric mixer, cream the butter until it is fluffy. Add the eggs and molasses and beat again for about 4 minutes. Add the figs, lemon peel, buttermilk, and pecans. Blend for 1 minute. Add the flour, baking soda, baking powder, salt, cinnamon, and cardamom.

NOTE: *Blend until everything is incorporated completely, but don't overmix! This is the number one cake problem; people keep beating and mixing until the cake is totally tough and overworked. Take it easy at this step!*

Pour the batter into the soufflé dish. Bake for 1 hour. If a toothpick inserted in the centre comes out clean, it's done. You can soak it in booze now and freeze it for later. Just don't forget the whipped cream when you're ready to serve!

CHRISTMAS MAINS

We always talk turkey at Christmastime, but I'm burnt out on it. I've spatchcocked the whole thing and had turkey on the table in 90 minutes. The overnight wet brine and the spicy dry brine? Been there, done those. I've roasted turkey until the skin was a gorgeous, dark, crackling caramel and served it along- side a chipotle gravy that you could drink straight from the ladle. Last year, after months of begging, I finally talked my family into letting me deep-fry the turkey. That event, however, came with conditions and provisions. I had to solemnly swear not to burn down my parents' house, while my sister's partner was appointed safety officer. Picture him, hovering around the steaming fryer, a beer in one hand and a fire extinguisher in the other, while my siblings looked on. Meanwhile, my husband was put in charge of the deep-fried turkey playlist and made everyone very nervous by blaring Alicia Keys's "Girl on Fire."

My beef with this monster bird? Well, it should be juicy and succulent, but more often than not it's dry and uninspiring. Most folks get nervous while roasting a turkey and they accidentally turn the whole thing dusty by roasting it much longer than needed. "Let's leave it in for another fifteen minutes" is often the death sentence of a decent meal. Plus, that carcass and those leftovers take up fridge real estate that should be reserved for peanut butter balls. Finally, I resent turkey because it is a bit of a culinary Stockholm-syndrome situation. Doing something just because we always have is the kind of logic that drives me batty. Traditions are living things that need to evolve, and some holiday meals might look unfamiliar and feel a bit different in the coming years, so we might as well shake things up. Without further ado, here are some alternative Christmas main courses for when a massive turkey doesn't make sense.

Stuffed Turkey Breast with Hazelnuts, Sage, and Whipped Goat's Cheese

MAKES ENOUGH FOR 2 TO 3 PEOPLE

Turkey breast stuffed with goat's cheese, dried sour cherries, breadcrumbs, hazelnuts, and sage gives a sense of pomp and occasion. Pair this with a gratin of winter greens, mashed potatoes, and a nice glass of Gamay, and you've got a lovely festive meal!

6 oz goat's cheese, softened

⅔ cup dried sour cherries or sun-dried tomatoes

1 cup cooked bacon, crumbled

⅔ cup hazelnuts, toasted and chopped

2 tsp chopped fresh sage

2 tsp fresh thyme, minced

Salt and pepper, to taste

¼ cup butter, softened

1 tbsp chopped fresh oregano

1 tbsp lemon zest

One 4-lb boneless turkey breast, skin on

Preheat oven to 400°F. Grease a large cast-iron pan or the bottom of a Dutch oven. **NOTE:** *Lining with parchment paper isn't necessary, but it will make clean-up easier.* In a medium-sized bowl mix together the goat's cheese, dried cherries, bacon, toasted hazelnuts, sage, and thyme until well combined. Season with salt and pepper and set aside. Mix together the butter, oregano, and lemon zest. Carefully lift the skin from the breast and spread a thin layer of the seasoned butter evenly underneath the skin. Lay the breast skin-side down and season with salt and pepper.

Now it's time to butterfly the turkey breast. Starting at the narrowest end of the meat, hold the blade of the knife parallel to your work surface. You'll need to make a horizontal cut about halfway through the thickness of the meat. Essentially, you're making two equally thick layers of turkey. Don't cut all the way through! Leave about three-quarters of an inch of meat along one edge.

Spread an even layer of the goat cheese mixture over the breast, leaving a half-inch border around its edge. Gently roll the turkey breast into a tight bundle and tie together with butcher's twine.

TIP > This is a skill that really worms its way into your brain when you watch someone else do it, so find a good YouTube tutorial.

Place the stuffed breast skin-side up in a roasting pan and place that on a lower oven rack. Roast for about 20 minutes. Turn down the oven temperature to 350°F and continue roasting for 45 minutes. Remove the roasted breast from the oven and let it rest in the pan for 15 minutes. Remove any twine and then carve the roast into ½-inch slices. Place desired amount on each serving plate and drizzle with pan juices.

Fried Oysters
from Merasheen, Newfoundland

MAKES ENOUGH FOR 2 TO 4 PEOPLE

I'm from PEI. My siblings and I are all seafood-obsessed. This means Christmas tends to come with a box of oysters, lemon, and hot sauce. Christmas morning involves someone scooping up snow and presenting the others with breakfast oysters on a little platter. One of us usually gets a new shucker in our stocking. My niece Cecily is a big seafood lover and there's something really satisfying about watching a five-year-old squeeze a little lemon onto her oyster, throw it down the hatch, and then clap her little hands together. This all might sound a little bourgeois, but it isn't. Oysters are very affordable on Prince Edward Island. You can throw a rock and hit an oyster farm. Someone usually "knows a guy" who can get a box at a decent price—not in an "illegal black market" way, but in a "my neighbour is an oyster farmer and he drops them off at the door" kind of way.

Newfoundland, however, is another story. The prices are much higher here and the oysters on sale have been shipped by air from other provinces, which doesn't jive with a desire to eat locally and doesn't exactly scream "fresh!" However, this all changed when Newfoundland started producing its own oysters. Merasheen Oyster Farms is producing gorgeous plump beauties. Ordering a box of local oysters is a great way to treat yourself in a year where treats have been sparse. I like raw oysters best, but when deep-fried they're a special treat!

Vegetable oil

2 large eggs

½ cup beer

1 tsp garlic salt

½ tsp lemon pepper

½ tsp onion powder

½ tsp garlic powder

Pinch cayenne pepper (optional)

2 cups flour

1 cup Panko

18 shucked oysters

1 lemon, sliced in wedges for garnish

I like to simply pan-fry these. Heat the oil in a deep pan to about 370°F. We're not using any exact measurements of oil: just pour it into the pan until it covers a few inches.

Take a nice big bowl and beat eggs, beer (I like to use a sour or an IPA), garlic salt, lemon pepper, onion powder, garlic powder, and cayenne together. Mix the flour and Panko in another bowl. Dip each oyster into the eggwash mixture, and then thoroughly roll it in the breadcrumbs. Arrange them on a sheet pan or cutting board— any flat surface will do— while you're dunking all of your oysters. Once all the oysters are prepped, fry them in the hot oil for 1 to 2 minutes per side, depending on the oyster's size, until they turn golden brown. **NOTE:** *Do not overcrowd the pan while frying.* Briefly drain on paper towels and serve while still hot. Garnish with lemon wedges.

I'd serve these on Christmas Eve with homemade fries and a good briny white wine.

Acorn Squash Stuffed with Vegan Pine-Nut Risotto

MAKES ENOUGH FOR 4 PEOPLE

Personally, I feel that stuffing a duck inside a turkey is a crime. Stuffing a vegetable with risotto, however, I can get behind! This squash is stuffed with a vegan pine-nut risotto. There's a bit of work involved, but I think it's worth the effort because your vegan friends usually have to make do with side dishes or bring their own tofurkey! Going the distance with this dish is a seasonal kindness. If you're just doing the vegetarian thing, then feel free to replace the vegan "Parmesan" with the real thing, or a good aged cheddar.

for the squash
2 acorn squashes (a smaller squash works well for this dish)

2 tbsp olive oil

Salt and pepper, to taste

¼ tsp red pepper flakes

for the pine-nut "butter"
1 cup pine nuts

2 tbsp olive oil

¼ cup cold water

Salt, to taste

for the vegan "Parmesan"
¾ cup raw cashews

3 tbsp nutritional yeast

1 tsp sea salt

¼ tsp garlic powder

to make the squash
Preheat oven to 400°F. Cut the squash in half and scrape out the seeds. Cut a small slice from the bottom of each squash half to create a stable surface for the "bowl." Rub the squash halves inside and out with olive oil, then sprinkle generously with salt and pepper. A few red pepper flakes at this stage adds a little base heat. Bake until the squash is gorgeous and caramelized, about 45 minutes, then set aside.

to make the pine-nut "butter"
Toast the pine nuts on the stovetop for a few minutes. **NOTE:** *The nuts should be hot but not browned; if they colour, it will make the risotto murky.*

Set a few of these aside as garnish. Put the rest of the pine nuts into a high-powered blender and blend with the olive oil and water until very smooth, stopping occasionally to scrape down the sides of the blender if needed. Season with salt. Set this mixture aside as well.

to make the vegan "Parmesan"
Add all ingredients to a food processor and mix/pulse until a fine meal is achieved. Store in the refrigerator to keep fresh. Lasts for several weeks.

for the risotto

2 tbsp olive oil

2 white onions, diced

1 cup arborio rice

3 cups vegetable stock

Salt, to taste

2 to 3 tbsp pine-nut "butter"

Herbs and sun-dried tomatoes, for garnish

¼ cup vegan "Parmesan"

to make the risotto

Heat the olive oil in a small pan and then gently sweat the onions until just soft but not coloured. Add the arborio rice and stir. Add one ladle of stock and cook, stirring constantly. When the stock has been absorbed, add another ladle of stock, still stirring. Continue this process, adding stock each time it is absorbed, until the rice is just cooked and the texture is like that of thick cream. Stir in 2 to 3 tablespoons of the pine-nut "butter" made previously, and continue stirring until thick and creamy. Once the risotto is ready, quickly transfer to the "bowl" of the acorn squash. Garnish with the pine nuts, herbs, some sun-dried tomatoes for colour and flavour, and vegan "Parmesan." Serve immediately.

SWEETS

THE FRUITCAKE DILEMMA

For many years, I hated fruitcake. Sure, I've given you a few recipes for Christmas cake, but it took a very long time to find a few recipes I actually enjoy. Hating fruitcake is not a very festive perspective, especially when you consider that many people think fruitcake is an essential element of the holiday season. I just did not understand the appeal for the longest time. Give me the sun-kissed peach pies of late summer, fresh berries doused in maple syrup, and apples tossed in sugar and cinnamon that have been roasted over a bonfire. Those are the desserts that I understand, but I cannot wrap my head around the idea of eating a cake that has the density of a dying sun.

I especially hate the mass-produced fruitcakes that you find in the grocery store aisles. Those terrible cakes are always covered in a fake buttercream, studded with radioactive green cherries, and drier than sawdust. To me, it seems like grocery store fruitcakes should be used as free weights or weapons, but should never, under any circumstances, be consumed. Not everyone shares my opinion. I posed a question on Facebook to try to gauge the popularity of the ubiquitous fruitcake, and things became heated. A friend from Quebec made a case for a cake that has been soaked in liquor for months. She argued that fruitcake is perfect for winter. It's sturdy, comforting, studded with candied fruits and toasted nuts—just what you need for long nights and cold winds. Others suggested that fruitcake is all about nostalgia and that the cake isn't so much about flavour, but about remembering the Christmases that have come before. Still others pointed out that some variation of fruitcake exists in many European cultures. England has its plum puddings, Italy has its panettone, and Germans begin the holiday season with stollen, which is like a yeasted fruitcake with ripples of marzipan throughout.

These are sound arguments, so I decided to take on the challenge of making friends with fruitcake. I wanted to work with two recipes—one rife with nostalgia, and the other packed with fruits, nuts, and booze. Surely between the two recipes, I could create an adaptation that would convert the most serious of fruitcake haters!

I began with Nan Hiscock's recipe. Nan Hiscock lives in Mount Pearl and is almost 100 years old. She has been making boiled raisin cakes, cherry cakes, and fruitcakes for over 80 years. She "retired" from baking at 95, but sometimes still gets in the spirit. Her grandson Daniel sent me a copy of her recipe.

To be honest, I wasn't sure about this. To begin with, the recipe called for margarine instead of butter and I love butter more than I love most anything. Daniel explained that the ingredients represent a time when butter was scarce and families needed to be economical about everything. These Christmas cakes symbolized the proud Newfoundland tradition of being able to make the most of tough times; in Nan Hiscock's case, this cake had to feed eleven children. With hesitation, I began baking Nan Hiscock's cake, and to be honest, I loved it. The cake was delicious. It was moister than expected and the recipe had the bonus of being simple and easy to follow.

Next, I embarked on a recipe sent to me by my friend Elodie. This was a cake in which the dried fruit was soaked in rum and whisky. It called for orange zest, dried apple, dried raisins, and apricots. The ingredient list was intimidating. I went to three different stores in order to pick up crystallized ginger and all the required spices. I was exhausted before I began, but oh, was it worth it! Every bite had perfect pitch; nutmeg and rum sang through the whole thing.

Ultimately, though, I felt there was something missing from both cakes. Nuts. Neither recipe called for the toasted nuts that I wanted, and while the first recipe was simple, the second was not. I want a fruitcake that can be whipped up easily, contains booze and nuts, and sends a nostalgic Christmas feeling throughout the house. After some testing, I developed a recipe that I think has something for everyone. Behold a fruitcake to change the mind of the fruitcake haters.

TIP > If you want to extend the life of your cake, keep it in the fridge, wrap it tight with plastic, and baste it with either port, bourbon, rum, or whisky daily.

The Most Perfect Fruitcake Recipe

MAKES ONE 9-INCH CAKE

for the dry fruit mixture
2 cups dried sour cherries

2 cups dried cranberries

½ cup candied citrus peel

1 cup pine nuts, toasted

1 cup walnuts, toasted

1 cup pecans, toasted

1 cup port

½ cup bourbon

¼ cup orange marmelade

for the cake
1 cup butter

1 ½ cups brown sugar

2 tbsp grated ginger

1 tsp lemon zest

1 tsp grapefruit zest

4 tbsp maple syrup

4 large eggs

2 ½ cups flour

2 tsp ground allspice

Pinch salt

for the hard sauce
1 cup butter, softened

2 cups icing sugar

2 ½ tbsp spiced rum

to make the dry fruit mixture
Combine all dry fruit and toasted nuts in a bowl. Add the booze and orange marmalade. Refrigerate for 24 hours minimum; longer is better. I soaked mine for 48 hours. Basically, we want the fruit to absorb all the liquid. Pour all the fruits and nuts into a pot and bring to a boil, and continue to boil until the fruits have sucked up all the liquid! Let cool completely.

to make the cake
Preheat oven to 300°F. Grease a 10-inch Bundt pan, or whatever 10-inch pan you choose, then line it with parchment paper. This is a sticky cake and you don't want your handiwork to be destroyed at the eleventh hour.

Using the paddle attachment of your stand mixer or a handheld mixer, cream together butter and sugar for 6 minutes, then add in your grated ginger, lemon zest, grapefruit zest, and maple syrup. Finally, beat eggs in one at a time. **NOTE:** *The mixture should look nice and smooth at this stage.* Add the remaining dry ingredients, taking care not to overmix. Now add the previously prepared fruit and nut mixture. Pour into the baking pan and cook for 2 hours or until done. Let cool before removing from pan. Serve with hard sauce.

to make the hard sauce
Beat the butter in your stand mixer until light and fluffy. Add the icing sugar slowly, so that it is fully incorporated. Scrape the sides of the bowl down as necessary. Slowly drizzle in the spiced rum. Spoon hard sauce into a bowl and keep at room temperature if using soon. If the meal is hours away, put the sauce in the fridge, but remove about an hour before use, as it hardens up and becomes difficult to loosen.

BEEHAK'S SHORTBREAD COOKIES

Beehak is one of the best pastry chefs I know, so I asked her for a recipe! Here it is in her own words:

This shortbread, like many of my frequently used recipes, has its origins in a Betty Crocker cookbook from the 1960s that lives in my mom's kitchen in Tehran. When I first got into baking as a teenager, the American approach to classic baked goods (homey, basic, not necessarily pretty but delicious) formed the foundation of my process. While I now enjoy making more complicated baked goods that might take days to prepare (hello, sourdough), I keep coming back to those basic principles. I've been using and altering this shortbread recipe for years, and have it boiled down to the absolute basics. I love the simplicity of it. With no leavening, complicated techniques, or long resting time, it's just about incorporating butter into flour and sugar, like a more sophisticated cousin of pie dough. Good shortbread is light and delicate and melts in your mouth. Even "bad" shortbread (tough, overworked, overbaked) is still buttery and delicious. The base recipe is a versatile canvas for flavours and textures. I've included some of my favourite variations below. Some recipe notes: to get the best results, keep the butter cold, don't overwork the dough, chill before baking, and know that parchment paper is your best friend for rolling out any kind of cookie dough. Living in Newfoundland is a blessing and a curse for baking. A lot of ingredients can be hard to track down or too expensive, but I also love that I can go for a walk with my dog and pick rose petals by the side of an urban trail—the city doesn't spray them with chemicals, despite popular belief. A longer hike can yield chuckley pear, blueberries, and cranberries, depending on the time of the year. Many of these foraged treasures can be incorporated into this recipe.

Shortbread Cookies

2 cups flour

1 cup confectioner's sugar

½ tsp salt

1 cup butter, cut into cubes and chilled

1 tsp vanilla (optional)

Pulse the dry ingredients together in a food processor to combine. Add vanilla, if using, and butter, and pulse until the dough comes together. Continue pulsing until the dough sticks together when pressed between two fingers. Scrape down the sides and under the blade to make sure it's evenly combined. Do not overmix. Turn the dough out onto a piece of parchment paper. Gently press together into a disk with your hands—do not knead. Cover with another piece of parchment paper and roll out to roughly

¼-inch thickness. Slide the rolled-out dough, still between the [sheets of] parchment paper, into the freezer for about 20 minutes, until firm.

Preheat oven to 350°F. Remove the dough from the freezer and remove the top sheet of parchment paper. Cut the cookies into squares or rectangles. They can be cut into a circle shape using a cookie cutter, but avoid more complicated shapes, as the dough is very "short" (crumbly); intricate shapes won't come out clean and will bake unevenly. Arrange the cookies 1 inch apart on the baking sheet. Do not grease the baking sheet, but if clean-up is a concern, you can line it with parchment paper.

Bake cookies for about 10 to 14 minutes, until the edges turn golden brown. Baking time will vary based on your oven and the size of the cookies, so keep an eye on them as they bake. Let the cookies cool on the baking sheet for 5 minutes after they come out of the oven, then move them to a cooling rack to cool completely. In theory, the baked cookies will keep for a week in an airtight container, but in practice they never last that long in my house!

VARIATIONS

Rose pistachio
Add 1 teaspoon of rosewater, a pinch of cardamom, and a handful of chopped, dried rose petals to the dough. After the dough comes together, add ⅓ cup roughly chopped raw pistachios and pulse to incorporate.

Chocolate-dipped orange
Add 1 ½ teaspoons orange zest to the dough. After baking, wait for the cookies to cool completely. Melt 1 cup semi-sweet chocolate chips in 20 second intervals in the microwave or in a double boiler over the stove. Dip the baked, fully cooled cookies in chocolate. Sprinkle with sea salt to finish.

Citrus berry
Add 1 ½ teaspoons orange or lemon zest to the dough. Add ⅓ cup chopped dried cranberries, blueberries, or chuckley pear after the dough comes together, and pulse to combine.

Espresso
Add 1 ½ teaspoons espresso powder or ground instant coffee to the dough.

Chocolate chip
Add ⅓ cup mini semi-sweet chocolate chips after the dough comes together, and pulse to combine.

CHRISTMAS SLUSH

I had my first taste of Christmas slush in Bay Roberts. Not wanting to be rude, I ignored my doubt and nodded when offered a glass.

The host proceeded outside to her deck, and came back in lugging a salt beef bucket. She ceremoniously placed the bucket in the centre of the kitchen table.

I calmly told myself the bucket had been thoroughly cleaned, surely. My glass was filled with 7-Up and then topped with an ice cream scoop's worth of slush. I was skeptical. The slush tasted like an orange cream popsicle—not a hint of beefiness, fortunately. It also packed a punch. The host later told me that she "puts all my leftover booze from the year into the slush." I'm surprised it was able to freeze!

This sweet drink is a proud bay tradition, but its origins are a bit of a mystery. Dale Jarvis, noted folklorist, had his own slush experience 'round the bay last Christmas: "I was trying to buy frozen lemonade, but every supermarket in town was out—everyone had bought it for slush." Jarvis suspects the tradition of slush comes from the British tradition of wassailing and may be connected to mummering. "The tradition of offering a visiting guest something rich and sweet to drink at Christmastime has existed in Newfoundland for decades and decades," Jarvis notes. However, the drink did not have to be boozy, says Jarvis. "We have this idea that Christmas drinks and mummering are connected to alcohol, but the Temperance movement was huge in some outports. Those communities enjoyed a drink called 'clingy,' and it was made from sweet syrups. Slush is probably derived from both of these traditions."

I wanted to know more about the history of this regional drink, but it is not directly connected to any historical records. Neither magazines nor newspaper articles make mention of it. I went through stacks of materials in libraries and archives trying to trace the history of this mysterious refreshment. Cookbook author Barry Parsons believes it was born in the 1980s. He remembers first trying it in Bonavista Bay in the early '80s, and soon after, it was everywhere! To him, it was a viral recipe before the internet. This makes sense to me. Slush does have the hallmark of 1980s recipes: sweet, neon, boozy, and often containing Jell-O powder, Cool Whip, or Tang. All of these signs point to the decade of excess.

Finally, I turned to crowdsourcing and social media, and asking people to share their slush recipes and opinions on the famous drink. Not a single person could tell me anything about the origin of the drinks, but most agreed if it wasn't served in a salt beef bucket then it didn't count as slush. "Gotta be a beef bucket" was a common response. Interestingly, a lot of people gendered the drink and mentioned that it was more of a tradition among moms and aunts than dads and uncles. Similarly, a number of my friends of were allowed to drink a single glass of slush at family gatherings when they were underage. Friends from different parts of the island sent me regional slush recipes. I was sent a Tetley Tea slush recipe from Grand Falls and rhubarb slush from Botwood; Barry Parsons sent me a link for his blueberry-partridgeberry slush, which admittedly looked delicious and a bit tonier than the others. Ultimately, I found a classic Creamsicle slush from the 1980s and adapted another recipe using damsons as well. Though I initially balked at the ingredients, the original recipe was simple to make and quite yummy. The real challenge will be saving it for the visitors.

Slush

MAKES ENOUGH TO FILL 1 SINGLE BELOVED SALT BEEF BUCKET

2 cans frozen orange juice, unsweetened

1 can frozen lemonade

1 cup sugar

6 cups water

1 cup Cool Whip brand imitation whipped cream (optional)

14 oz vodka (optional)

Lemon lime pop, ginger ale or club soda to serve with it

Mix all ingredients except pop in a large mixing bowl. Stir very thoroughly. Transfer to an exceptionally clean salt beef bucket and freeze for 24 hours. Stir a few times during the first 6 hours in order to achieve the proper slushy texture. Serve the slush over a glass of pop.

NOTE: *Cool Whip and vodka are optional. Lots of people just use whatever booze they have lying around; vodka simply impacts the flavour the least. Cool Whip is a crime against humanity, in my opinion, and I would never normally advocate for its use, but in this one particular instance, it serves a purpose and adds a creamy smooth mouth feel to the whole thing. I think the slush goes best with ginger ale, but most people prefer 7-Up.*

REFERENCES

LATE WINTER TO EARLY SPRING

Versions of the lassy bread recipe on page 23 show up in different Newfoundland cookbooks and church notebooks under different names, but you can find this version on page 56 of *Fat-Back and Molasses*. This book is a great resource for recipes from Newfoundland and Labrador and is, in my opinion, a must-have for any cookbook enthusiast.

Potato pancakes and rolls pop up all over, but my recipe on page 28 is a combination of potato pancake recipes mostly inspired by the Presbyterian Ladies' Aid (P.L.A.) cookbooks, including the 1924 edition of this title:

The P.L.A. Cook Book: arranged from tried and proven recipes, by St. Andrew's Presbyterian Church (St. John's, NL) Ladies' Aid Society. St. John's: Ladies' Aid Society of St. Andrew's Presbyterian Church, 1939.

On page 22 I mention a bread-baking competition in Carbonear that took place in 1939. You can find that article in the *Daily Telegram* from April 17, 1939. There are also ads for this same competition posted in local newspapers printed throughout the month.

Ginger cakes and gingerbreads can be found in many older Newfoundland cookbooks, but these two on page 38 were found in the *Ladies' College Aid Society Cookbook*. Written in 1905, this beautiful old recipe book can be found in the Provincial Archives at The Rooms in St. John's. The gingerbread recipes came from page 81.

The lobscouse recipe on page 42 comes from my mother-in-law, Linda Warford, who is not fond of cooking, but learned some great recipes at the hands of a master—Nan Warford, *her* mother-in-law. Similar recipes exist all over.

Pea soup recipes abound too, but the one on page 44 comes from the 1938 edition of the P.L.A. cookbook mentioned above. The dough boy/dumpling recipe, however, is a combination of recipes that I tested and liked.

The baked turr recipe on page 53 was found in the *Catalina Volunteer Fire Department Cookbook*. No publication date was given anywhere in this book.

MID-SPRING TO SUMMER

The recipe for steamed dandelion greens on page 89 and the cod au gratin recipe on page 138 were found in the *Newfoundland Cookbook: Newfoundland Dishes for You to Enjoy Back Home*, published and distributed by Macy's Publishing Co. in St. John's, in 1973.

The recipe for "Pommes De Terre Au Gratin" on page 120 came from the third edition of the P.L.A. Cook Book, published in 1939.

The jellied beet salad found on page 121, which I've called "Old-School Beet Salad," can be found in *A Souvenir Cookbook of Fogo Island NFLD*. There was no publication date listed, but it appears to be from the 1970s.

"Turnip Treat," a recipe from *Corner Brook's Favorite Recipes*, published by Bentley Club, First United Church in 1941 and reprinted in 1960, can be found on page 126 of this book.

On page 127, the interesting parsnip ball recipe also came from *Corner Brook's Favorite Recipes*. "Parsnip Balls" were original to the first printing of this cookbook in 1941.

I amalgamated recipes and created my own version of classic rhubarb chutney (page 111), but a similar version can be found on page 82 of *Caribou Cakes: Reflections and Recipes of Labrador Food*.

The second cod au gratin recipe in this book was inspired by Barry Parsons's version, which can be found in *Rock Recipes: The Best Food from My Newfoundland Kitchen*, by Barry C. Parsons, published by Breakwater Books in 2014.

AUTUMN

The blueberry cake recipe on page 158 comes from the *Ladies' College Aid Society Cookbook*, written in 1905. The recipe was written by a Mrs. G. Milligina.

The breakfast apple recipe on page 170 came from a newspaper clipping tucked in a little recipe book that had been donated to the Provincial Archives at The Rooms. It was from a local newspaper from 1934, but I was unable to figure out which newspaper.

On page 176, the pumpkin marmalade recipe comes from page 155 of *Sharing My Best: The Classic Cookbook of Newfoundland Recipes*, by Shirley Wornell, published by Flanker Press in 2004. You can find a very similar pumpkin marmalade recipe on page 58 of the *Twillingate Times*, which was published in 1981.

Colcannon Night (page 182) is mentioned in the St. John's newspaper the *Evening Telegram* on November 1, 1902. Recipes for colcannon are given in a whack of old cookbooks and it's spelled differently each time, but I like the version in *Corner Brook's Favorite Recipes*.

CHRISTMAS

"Stir-Up Sunday," as described on page 208, is mentioned in a column in the *Daily News* on November 23, 1956. I also read more about "Stir-Up Sunday" through this website: https://www.historic-uk.com/CultureUK/Stir-Up-Sunday.

Nan Hiscock's recipe, as described on page 221, was written on a piece of paper with tons of marginalia scribbled on it. Her grandson Daniel Hiscock connected me with her recipe.

I didn't use recipes from the following books, but did find them informative, helpful, and—in the case of the Sprung Greenhouse cucumber cookbook—just plain weird. Bibliographic information is scarce or entirely lacking for some titles; I've provided what was available.

Our favorite recipes. St. Philip's Anglican Church Women's Association (Nfld.). St. John's: Dicks & Co., [1974?].

Cucumber recipes from Newfoundland Enviroponics. Presented by Beverly Sprung. [1988?].

Caribou Cakes: Reflections and Recipes of Labrador Food. Them Days Magazine, Happy Valley-Goose Bay, Labrador: Them Days, 2000.

Clarissa Lodlow (Fogo) daybook, 1899–1929. Collection MG956, Item MG956.213, found at The Rooms Provincial Archives.

Diary of a Trip to Labrador, June-August 1925. Fonds MG 186, Item MC 186.1, also found at The Rooms Provincial Archives.

Twillingate Times: A Collection of Oldtime Recipes and Folklore from Twillingate, Newfoundland, 1981.

United Church Girls' Club Cook Book by First United Church, Corner Brook, NL. Girls' Club Corner Brook, NL, printed by the *Western Star,* 1948.

Favorite recipes Bake Apple Folk Festival, 1989.

INDEX